THE
MARRIAGE
MANUAL

THE
MARRIAGE
MANUAL

Ten Checkpoints
For Peak Performance

by

Duane Cuthbertson

HORIZON HOUSE PUBLISHERS
Beaverlodge, Alberta, Canada

ISBN 0-88965-038-1

HORIZON BOOKS
are published by Horizon House Publishers
Box 600, Beaverlodge, Alberta TOH OCO
Printed in the United States of America

Dedication

This book belongs to many people. It belongs to my wife Marilyn and our five children, whose inspiration and perspiration have made it possible.

It belongs to Louise Harkaway who has typed the manuscript four times. She knows the material well. Any questions can be directed to her.

It belongs to Glenn Gilbert who contributed his journalism skills and helped in the editing.

The book belongs to you. Thank you from all of us for the invitation to enter your home.

Mostly it belongs to God. Any seedlings of truth and wisdom are His. Thank you, Father.

Duane Cuthbertson

Contents

Introduction / 9
Foreword / 11

1. **Who's at the Wheel?**
   Roles of Husband and Wife / 13

2. **What's Under the Hood?**
   Complexity of Relationships / 33

3. **Blowing Your Horn**
   Communication In Marriage / 45

4. **Checking the Oil**
   The Lubrication of Love / 61

5. **Tuning the Engine**
   The Energy Source of Your Marriage / 79

6. **Avoiding Collisions**
   Will Vs. Will Confrontation / 91

7. **Watching Those Gauges**
   Dealing With Pressures / 109

8. **Keeping the Revs Up**
   Sex In Marriage / 125

9. **Those Back Seat Speakers**
   The Psychology of Raising Children / 141

10. **Shifting Gears**
    Keeping Up With Your Teens / 161

Introduction

Here is a book that combines biblical insight, proven psychological principles and a good deal of face-to-face experience with people over a number of years. It has been my privilege to enjoy the friendship and counsel of Duane Cuthbertson and to profit personally from his ministry.

There are many books written on the subject of marriage today. Many of them offer fine insights from a theoretical standpoint; others are very interesting reading because of the strength of their anecdotes. This book has both. Duane gives us no easy formulas, nor does he generalize off of specific situations. Instead, he displays a basic attitude that is carefully aligned with the Word of God.

It has long been my opinion that if the enemy of our souls wanted to truly subvert God's world, and indeed he does, he would aim at the most central unit, the family. I am equally confident that God is aware of this and would not ask us to do something that is impossible. Therefore, He has put us together as husbands and wives in families and provided for us the principles of His Word, both in the organization of the family and in the interrelationships within the family that maximize our prospects of success and happiness. Those who have raised families or are raising families will be touched deeply by the sensitivity and completeness of the man/wife relationship separate from the function of parenthood. Those who are young and looking forward toward marriage will find this book a useful road map revealing some well marked pitfalls to avoid in the pathway of married life.

Jay Kesler

Foreword

We've all had the frustration of just **not** being able to get that car started. It seems the more we try, the more we flood the engine. There are intricate mechanical **principles** that must function cooperatively and accurately if we are to have success.

This is not only true in applied science, but also in life as a whole. If we apply correct **principles** to our lives and to our marriages, we will have harmony. If not, we will have dissonance. This can be a simple but profound "barometer."

There are two types of "happy" people. Those who were raised "in it" and those who had to "learn it." If happiness, security, and stability are your goals, it is good to learn and practice these qualities, until they finally become you. Since most of our homes are inconsistent, the natural, absolute flow of joy is impaired. Even the apostle Paul in Philippians 4:11 had "...**learned** in whatever state he was therewith to be content." There are two encouraging conclusions: first, he too had to work at it, and second, he found it and was content.

God is obviously attempting to move us through a process. He wants us to be "complete" (Matthew

5:48). Our part is to apply the **principles** of His word to our lives and to our relationships. II Peter 1:4 states, "Whereby are given unto us exceeding great and previous **promises**, that we might be partakers of His Divine Nature, having escaped the corruption in this world through lust." Thus, the goal is to have a life that is led by **principle** and not emotion.

As your automobile has "parts" and each must function properly for success, so the marriage contract is equally complex. I challenge you to follow this anaolgy and learn new **principles** about the various areas of your marriage. As you apply them, God through His Spirit and His Word **will** recharge your battery.

Duane Cuthbertson

1

Who's at the Wheel?

Roles of Husband and Wife

A marriage relationship demands adjustment. A Scripture that always brings a smile to my lips is Deuteronomy 24:5, "When a man hath taken a new wife, he shall not go out to war, neither shall he be charged with any business: but he shall be free at home one year, and shall cheer up his wife which he hath taken."

He shall cheer her up. What a smile. Is he to entertain with jokes and anecdotes? Obviously not. At this point I will just tease you into conjecture as to what it really means, but certainly to the early Jewish civilization the first year of marriage was important. The couple was literally isolated. The community supported them.

Not so today! Now we run off for a week or so and return to reality with all of the stress and pressures...adjusted. Many not only have no honeymoon, but many couples never do manage to adjust.

Thus, as we bring ourselves into marriage, we also bring our strengths and weaknesses. **We can never**

13

go on the premise that our parents did it right.

You as a husband, you as a wife, must have a clearly defined idea of your role to one another. Our society today in large measure suggests that this role is subjective. Couples are expected to define it individually. Without apology, I would suggest that these roles have been defined in the Word of God, the Bible.

After a conference meeting one evening, a man came to me in tears. "I have six children. My two teenagers are on drugs. My wife and I argue and fight constantly. We are in the process of a divorce," he related.

He was successful by our world's standards. He headed a small engineering firm with twenty men working under him. There was the big house, the big cars, the big problems.

"Where did you get your training to become an engineer?" I inquired.

"Well, I went to college for a B.S. degree, then received an M.A. from the University of Michigan," he responded.

As the conversation continued, I gently asked, "And where did you get your education to become a father or husband?"

I think he felt that he had been hit by a two-by-four.

You, my friend, where did you learn to become a father, a mother, a husband, a wife? It's sobering to grasp that for most of us, it has to be learned.

The Bible states in Galatians 6:7, "Be not deceived. God is not mocked. Whatsoever a man soweth that shall he also reap." If I take my automobile and accelerate to a speed of 70 m.p.h. and then run it into a telephone pole, because I have violated certain basic laws of physics, in every sense I will pay for it.

14

This is also true in our homes. If we follow God's principles, things will fall into place. If not, we will pay for it.

How I appreciate the passage in Proverbs 1:23-33. It mentions three positive results of real wisdom, and then three negative results.

The three positive results are found in 1:23, 33. "Turn you at my reproof: behold, I will pour out my spirit unto you, I will make known my words unto you." "But whoso harkeneth unto me shall dwell safely, and shall be quiet from fear of evil."

(1.) He will pour out his spirit to us; (2.) he will make known his words to us; and (3.) we shall be quiet from fear of evil. It is shattering to realize that as God in His sovereignty becomes personal, the end result is quietness within. Subconsciously we all strive for an inner peace and inner freedom. We can have it. It can be ours.

The three negative results are listed in Proverbs 1:26, 27 and 32. "I also will laugh at your calamity; I will mock when your fear cometh; When your fear cometh as desolation, and your destruction cometh as a whirlwind; when distress and anguish cometh upon you...For the turning away of the simple shall slay them, and the prosperity of fools shall destroy them." These negative results are (1.) inner calamity, (2.) much fear, and (3.) eventual destruction. As man rejects God and God's principles, disorganization, struggles, anxieties, fears, diffusion and much calamity will come into his life. Anyone relate?

Perhaps a couple of the wisest statements we make are, "I don't know" and "I don't understand." In the true sense, we all lack knowledge, we are all ignorant. The ambitious goal of this chapter is to help you to understand. The worst problems in homes are caused by either sheer ignorance (lack of understanding of Biblical principles), or a direct, willing violation of God's principles. If I choose to violate a principle that I understand, it is obviously a matter of my own will.

There are underlying principles that I would like to share. Please recognize that there are three passages concerning roles which you need to study and make yours: I Peter 3:1-7, Ephesians 5:21-31, and Proverbs 31:15-31. "For this cause shall a man leave father and mother and shall cleave to his wife, and they shall be one flesh" (Ephesians 5:31). **The goal of your marriage should be oneness.**

Do you ever ask, "For what cause?" The principle is clear—the husband is to leave father and mother and cleave to his wife. But notice the first phrase—"For this cause..." For what cause? Back up one verse and you will see that the preceding verse relates to the concept of the Church. "For we are members of His body, of His flesh and of His bones." Therefore, the underlying principle is built upon the idea of two people losing their identities and becoming one within the body of Christ. This seems to be an expansion of the early Mosaic concept in Genesis 2:24. As I write, she writes. When my wife is home with our five children, I am there too. We are "heirs together of the grace of life" (I Peter 3:7). Any success or failure my wife has as she ministers to the children or that I have ministering in conferences is a joint effort. We are together. As the Church is to be unified, so is the home to reflect a oneness.

Folks sometimes say, "They have been married so long they almost look alike." What a compliment!

The process is working. The identification is such that the "oneness" is obvious.

Whatever we are within the body of Christ, the Church of Christ, we should be together. Therefore, I challenge you to analyze if there is this type of spiritual union in your marriage.

It takes only two people to initiate a difference of opinion. When I first attended college, I was the prankster...water above the door, short sheets.... One night my roommate and I went out for a hamburger and when we returned, I turned the doorknob only to have the door fall to the floor. My dorm friends not only had taken the door off the hinges, but every item in the room had been removed. No clothes, no dressers, no toothbrushes, nothing! We spent the rest of the evening going door to door throughout the entire dorm trying to retrieve our belongings.

God bless them. That type of crisis now brings a smile. But **a crisis in marriage can either draw a couple closer together or drive the couple apart**.

As I shall soon share in the chapter on love, a verse in Song of Solomon states, "Many waters cannot quench love, neither can the floods drown it" (8:7). There will be waters; there will be floods, Remember. it is not **what** happens. It is how you interpret what happens.

"Never a problem, just an opportunity."

If we can view crises as times of refinement and growth, and genuinely praise the Lord that He is helping us to define certain areas, as strange as it might seem to others around, we can welcome crises. We know the result will be growth.

Our wisdom is limited, but God wants us to develop it (Proverbs 2:6, 7). He has wisdom "laid up" for us.

17

A crisis in marriage, then, manifests our helplessness, and we should indeed find ourselves in prayer, seeking God's guidance. I recently counselled a couple who had been fighting constantly for 37 years. They never learned how to deal with crises.

If you will pardon the poor English, let's start with the husband since I "are" one.

The husband is to initiate love. In our society this is almost paradoxical. It is harder for a man to experience love, but Biblically the responsibility rests on him. And where do I learn to love? What if there was little love in my background? What if I came off the streets of Detroit, Chicago or New York? What if all I knew was aggression, hate and hostility?

The Bible relates, "Husbands, love your wives as Christ also loved the Church" (Ephesians 5:25). It also tells the husband to live with his wife "according to knowledge" (I Peter 3:7). Biblically, the emphasis of love rests upon the husband. Interesting. God is aware that it is much harder for a man to experience and express love. He generally doesn't have any problem understanding sex; he generally doesn't have any problem understanding security. But he has a great deal of difficulty in the breaking process necessary to understand love.

When I was in high school, I played football. After beating my head against someone else's for a couple of hours, I was expected to shower down with a bunch of rough and ready guys in the locker room, and then go out on a date. On this date I was to open the door, help a young lady into the car, help her with a chair, and have an entirely different image. I was suddenly to be sweet, tender and loving. A man, then, has to go through a breaking process if he is to understand love. Peter was never the same after the cock had crowed three times. He was broken. Many of us do not realize that God takes us through irritations and difficulties to move us into a breaking process. Then we are ready to love.

"Likewise ye husbands, dwell with them according to knowledge, giving honor unto the wife as unto the weaker vessel" (I Peter 3:7). The "weaker vessel" concept has stimulated a great deal of controversy. I suggest it has nothing to do with physical strength. I suppose if it came to a drag 'em out, knock 'em down fight, most husbands are stronger than their wives. Most men are structurally made to be physically stronger (there are exceptions).

But frankly, when it comes to having children, I am sure I speak for most males in saying that we are perfectly willing to leave that whole area to the ladies. I think women do a very fine job and there is great wisdom in the saying, "If the wife had the first child and the husband had the second child, there would be no third child."

The "weaker vessel" does not relate to the physical. It refers to an attitude that a husband should have toward his wife. Notice it says "as unto a weaker vessel," or to treat her as if she were such. It is an attitude, a basic ingredient involved in this breaking process. Perhaps the best way to illustrate it is this. I have a niece who is retarded. She is approximately seventeen years of age, but in mental development she is less than a year old. This dear girl is incapable of feeding herself, she has no knowledge of her parents, and it wrings my heart to visit her. Society has said, "This is a weaker vessel." If that little retarded girl were in our presence and I began to scream at her or abuse her in any way, you men would have my hide, and rightly so. She is incapable of defending herself—she is a weaker vessel! I am to initiate love toward her. I am to give her love as if I do not expect love in return. That precisely is the weaker vessel concept. And men, that is exactly the attitude you should have in your mind toward your wife—to initiate love as if you are not going to receive love in return. Very, very few men have come to a point in life where they can even begin to understand the psychological dynamics of this type of attitude.

Staggering as this responsibility is, **the husband is to be the teacher in the family also.** Obviously this is not all inclusive; both parents teach. The point is one of emphasis.

How can we measure the hundreds of hours David must have spent with Solomon? Solomon concluded, "For I was my father's son, tender and only beloved in the sight of my mother. He taught me also, and said unto me, Let thine heart retain my words, keep my commandments and live. Get wisdom, get understanding; forget it not; neither decline from the words of my mouth" (Proverbs 4:3-5).

"He taught me also."

Do you men remember when your dad said, "Let me show you how to run that saw...Here's the way you hold the paint brush." Subconsciously, they were teaching. Those swear words, the cheating on the income tax, the beer bottles, these are also examples of teaching—bad teaching. "You go on to church. I think I'll play a round of golf."

Dad, your children learn by what you are. It is sobering. I remember sitting at the dinner table one

20

night and being very tired, I breathed a deep sigh and said to my wife, "Oh, dear." Within five minutes one of our little girls looked over and without even thinking about it breathed a sigh and said, "Oh dear." I looked at my wife and winked because I had suddenly become aware of this principle. You can never expect your children to be something you are not. Sometimes God in His grace allows that to happen, but we cannot count on it. If you were to reproduce yourself spiritually in your children, what type of people would they be? If your children were to come to you and ask you about God, Jesus Christ, God's Word, would you have an answer for them, or would you say, "Go ask your mother?" Do you know what you believe or what you are spiritually?

A classic illustration relates how a father left his home during a bad snowstorm to go to the neighborhood bar. Halfway there, he turned to see his boy playing the game "walk in Daddy's tracks" as the imprints of his boots were left in the snow. As he observed his son attempting to jump from step to step, the sobering reality was that "he was walking in Dad's steps." And Dad, he does. I not only affect my children, but my children's children. My attitudes affect my grandchildren. Proverbs 13:22, "A good man leaves an inheritance to his children's children." Proverbs 17:6, "Children's children are the crown of old men: and the glory of children are their fathers."

My wife used to compare me to my father-in-law. He is good mechanically and frankly, I am not. I have a hunch that many of you have gone through such comparisons. But you gals are perceptive. When we are first married no one can make pumpkin pie like

21

"Mom". Then after ten years of marriage our wives make the best pumpkin pie in the world.

But really, I am aware that every time my wife makes a comparison she really is complimenting her father. She was her father's "son" because they had no boys. Probably my grandchildren will be weak mechanically because I will pass little mechanical ability on to my son, but I do believe my boy will have something for his children psychologically and spiritually. He might not sit down with his children and present the three points of the role of a husband in marriage, but I hope the impact of his father will be there in terms of stability and security.

Thirdly, Dad, **realize that you set the emotional tone in your home**. Proverbs 11:29 declares, "He that troubleth his own house shall inherit the wind, the fool shall be the servant of the wise in heart." There **is** an emotional tone in your home. There is an atmosphere in every home. Is it described with words like love, warmth, and joy? Or hostility, anger, and bitterness? What words would you use to characterize your house? Do you come home expecting things to function around you or are you able to manifest a spirit of love? Many of us have to bite our tongues because we give ourselves to wrath much more easily than to appeasement. Proverbs 15:18 says, "A wrathful man stirreth up strife, but he that is slow to anger appeaseth strife." The strength is not found in the loudness of your voice, but in your ability to appease. The last part of I Peter 3:7 says, "...that your prayers be not hindered." This means that I can pray for my children until I run out of breath, but if I am not willing to attempt to follow God's principles it will be to no avail. My prayers will go no higher than the ceiling. We reap what we sow. "Be not deceived, God is not mocked, Whatsoever a man soweth, that shall he also reap" (Galatians 6:7).

I trust, men, this analysis is meaningful. What are you like when you are home? Some people are great at work and great at church, but when they get home the real person slips through. I could relate experience after experience in which teenagers have told me, "My dad is a hypocrite. He is a deacon at church but you should see him at home." Or, "My dad is a pastor...." In some cases violations of Biblical principles are obvious, but in others it is a case of letting the temperament or the flesh supercede what God meant the father to be.

Finally, **the husband is leader**. Please note that from a Biblical base, he **is** leader. If you happen to come from a maternally dominant home, recognize that this is the way Dad chose to lead. This concept is under fire today. The major Scripture is Ephesians 5:21-31:

> Submitting yourselves one to another in the fear of God. Wives, submit yourselves unto your own husbands, as unto the Lord. For the husband is the head of the wife, even as Christ is the head of the church: and he is the savior of the body. Therefore as the church is subject unto Christ, so let the wives be to their own husbands in every thing. Husbands, love your wives, even as Christ also loved the church, and gave himself for it; That he might sanctify and cleanse it with the washing of water by the word, That he might present it to himself a glorious church, not having spot

23

or wrinkle, or any such thing: but that it should be holy and without blemish. So ought men to love their wives as their own bodies. He that loveth his wife loveth himself. For no man ever yet hated his own flesh; but nourisheth and cherisheth it, even as the Lord the church: For we are members of his body, of his flesh, and of his bones. For this cause shall a man leave his father and mother, and shall be joined unto his wife, and they two shall be one flesh. This is a great mystery but I speak concerning Christ and the church. Nevertheless let every one of you in particular so love his wife even as himself; and the wife see that she reverence her husband.

This passage compares a husband-wife relationship to the Christ-Church relationship. The graphics deal with the human body. We each have a head and a body. Profound, I know. Scripture relates to Christ being the head of the Church; the Church is set forth as the body. Ephesians 4:15-15, "But speaking the truth in love, may grow up into him in all things which is the head, even Christ: from whom the whole body fitly joined together and compacted by that which every joint supplies, according to the effectual working of the measure of every part, maketh increase of the body unto the edifying of itself in love." Christ is the leader and all have a function within the body. Christ is the shepherd (John 10); He cares for the body (us—the Church). Now, read Ephesians 5:21-31 again.

What a tender relationship of the head (husband), leading, yes, but caring for the body (wife). We

24

should function as Christ (Ephesians 5:23). Love our wives, as Christ loved the Church (5:25). The passage I especially like is verse 26. "That he might sanctify and cleanse it with the washing of water by the word." When you take a bath, it is the head that directs the hands where to clean. What a tender, loving responsibility—leading the wife. We are to develop the wife to be holy and without blemish. In essence this means my wife should be a better person being married to me. My task is to help develop her potential. **My leadership is measured by the growth pattern of my wife.** If I am president of a bank, head of a corporation, pastor of a church, but my wife's spiritual and psychological individuality has been stymied by my poor leadership, I have failed as a leader.

Without much transition, let's analyze the role of the wife in marriage. The most misunderstood concept concerning the Christian wife is **her role to submit organizationally**.

"Wives, be in subjection to your own husbands; that if any obey not the word, they also may without the word be won by the behavior of their wives" (I Peter 3:1). This is God's way of resolving conflict. It is a good place for us to begin; it relates to the very fiber of the home. How do you resolve conflicts in your home? If a difference of opinion arises, what do you do? Scream? Cry? Can you sit down and objectively work through your differences? Even those of you who are mature enough to be able to sit down and logically work through differences know that eventually there must be flexibility by someone. And after an individual conflict has been resolved, both of you know who ended up getting his/her way. God established this type of pattern. This does not mean the husband is the "boss." In fact, if the husband has to make such innuendos, he is violating the principles God set forth concerning his role. You are not the boss. You do not tell your wife what to do!

Women, it is as practical as this: if there is a difference of opinion, God does not necessarily expect you to agree with your husband. You are an individual and have every right to your own opinion and your independence. But I think God's pattern calls for you to say, "Honey, I do not agree with you, but if that is what you feel, that is what we will do." You are thereby allowing your husband to be the head of the home. Many times husbands want to be the heads of their homes but are not allowed to be such. In other cases, husbands are incapable of being the heads of their homes. Wives, you can best reinforce the potential of your husbands' capabilities of assuming the headship of the home through your own attitude. Carl Jung states, "Where love rules there is no will to power."

Proverbs 31 establishes the ideal attributes of the Christian wife. She goes out and buys land without consultation from her husband, she is industrious, compassionate, sets up a schedule of her day, etc.:

> Who can find a virtuous woman? for her price is far above rubies. The heart of her husband doth safely trust in her, so that he shall have no need of spoil. She will do him good and not evil all the days of her life. She seeketh wool, and flax, and worketh willingly with her hands. She is like the merchants' ships; she bringeth her food from afar. She riseth also while it is yet night and giveth meat to her

household, and a portion to her maidens. She considereth a field, and buyeth it: with the fruit of her hands she planteth a vineyard. She girdeth her loins with strength, and strengtheneth her arms. She perceiveth that her merchandise is good: her candle goeth not out by night. She layeth her hands to the spindle, and her hands hold the distaff. She stretcheth out her hand to the poor; yes, she reacheth forth her hands to the needy. She is not afraid of the snow for her household: for all her household are clothed with scarlet. She maketh herself coverings of tapestry; her clothing is silk and purple. Her husband is known in the gates, when he sitteth among the elders of the land. She maketh fine linen, and selleth it; and delivereth girdles unto the merchant. Strength and honor are her clothing; and she shall rejoice in time to come. She openeth her mouth with wisdom; and in her tongue is the law of kindness. She looketh well to the ways of her household, and eateth not the bread of idleness. Her children rise up, and call her blessed; her husband also, and he praiseth her. Many daughters have done virtuously, but thou excellest them all. Favor is deceitful and beauty is vain; but a woman that feareth the Lord, she shall be praised. Give her the fruit of her hands; and let her own works praise her in the gates.

How many of you women would go out and buy real

estate without your husband's awareness? Frankly, men, we come off pretty poorly. While the wife is actively involved, notice where "Dad" is. "Her husband is known in the gates, when he sitteth among the elders of the land." Note her wisdom in letting him lead. "She openeth her mouth with wisdom; and in her tongue is the law of kindness."

How much wisdom and kindness come forth when you talk? Many of us would have to go through drastic reformations of our personalities to suddenly have wisdom and be endowed with a natural kindness. You can never assume that the way your parents did things was right. Many times our parents may not have known the principles of God's Word. Dissect your words and consider the spirit in which they are spoken. Notice that the wife in Proverbs 13 "looketh well in the ways of her household and eateth not the bread of idleness." I think our housekeeping does reflect upon our ability to understand what God's Word has for us.

I personally believe a woman's happiness is found through her husband and through her children. "Her children rise up and call her blessed and her husband also" (Proverbs 31:28). When a mother can look back over her life knowing that this is the way her husband and her children feel about her, she is successful.

Women, you know you have the ability to either build or destroy your home. In large measure, if the home collapses emotionally or psychologically, the responsibility lies with the wife. Of course, this is not inclusive. I Peter 3:2 and I Corinthians 6:14 present what a godly mother and wife can do in changing the attitudes of her husband and her children. But many women simply are too human. Crises arise and they

28

collapse. The qualities of strength, honor and wisdom disappear.

If your husband seems to have "lost his first love," if your children seem to have changed, if your marriage seems to be fading, why? Women have the option of building or destroying homes. If a woman has the perception, she can take the problems that come on a day-by-day basis and use them as building blocks. Or the woman can take the problems and become bitter, resentful and hateful.

A mother can build in a number of ways. She can build by **her attitude, her communication, and her creativity.** The wise woman sees every opportunity as a building block, and she envisions her home five years in the future. It is a matter of wisdom.

We have some very dear friends, and to be honest with you, the wife is much more intelligent than her husband. However, it is beautiful to see them interact. If you ask them a question that she could answer quickly, she will look to her husband and let him lead.

He digs for words...she will say nothing and let him answer in minutes questions to which she could respond in 30 seconds. She is wise. There is no loss of individuality. She loves him and she is wise.

The two final battlefields are usually the pocketbook and the bed. Sex can be used by the wife as a wedge. In situation after situation husbands and wives can be found who no longer occupy the same bed. Perhaps this is because the wife has chosen to destroy rather than to build.

"Let her be as the loving hind and pleasant roe. Let her breasts satisfy thee at all times, and be thou ravished always with her love. And why wilt thou, my son, be ravished with a strange woman, and embrace the bosom of a stranger?'' (Proverbs 5:19-20).

In the Scriptures, the "thread" most obvious for the husband deals with his emotional leadership, his ability to love. For the wife God drives deeply into her inner stability. She should have **a quiet spirit**. I Peter 3:4, "But let it be the hidden man of the heart, in that which is not corruptible, even the ornament of **a meek and quiet spirit**, which is in the sight of God of great price."

Please note the two characteristics—meekness and quietness. In many homes we have just the opposite. Our society lauds arrogance and loudness. We feel we have to be independent and strong-willed to survive. What a pity!

Solomon says, "It is better to live in the wilderness than with an angry and contentious woman" (Proverbs 21:19). Angry and contentious women are irrational. They have no desire to decide conflicts or work toward resolution. They only have a desire to spill out the venom they have inside. God wants women to have meek and quiet spirits. And men are drawn to these characteristics as well.

Women, what are you like? Are you driving your husbands into the wilderness?

Let's make a brief summary. Husbands, be aware that you must submit emotionally, establish the right tone in your home and be a good teacher and leader. Be aware that you are affecting generations to come. Also, treat your wife as if she were a weaker vessel.

Wives, are you submitting organizationally? Do you really understand what it means to use words of wisdom and kindness, and to have meek and quiet spirits? Are you building or destroying your home?

One of the most profound statements I have ever

heard came up during "questions and answers" at a family life conference. I had raised the question, "What is your conclusion to what has been said?"

A woman responded, "Duane, I am convinced that there is not a woman alive who would not be willing to submit organizationally to her husband if she had a husband who was willing to submit emotionally to her."

What a truth! There must be two people who understand Biblical principles and are willing to say, "This is the best. This is what we will establish and work toward."

Questions - Test Yourself

1. A crisis in marriage will either _draw closer_ or _draw apart_.

2. A key verse for married couples to have as their own is Song of Solomon 8:7, which states, "Many _Waters_ cannot quench love, neither can the _flood_ drown it."

3. The basic responsibility of a husband in marriage is to give and initiate _Love_.

4. The "weaker vessel" concept is found in the Bible in _I Pet. 3:7_

5. Besides initiating love, two other principles that are part of the responsibility of the husband are _Teacher Leader_ and _Set Emotional Tone_.

6. It is the responsibility of _MeN_ to set the right emotional tone for the home (Proverbs 11:29).

7. The basic responsibility of the wife in marriage is to submit _Organizationally_.

8. Wives being in submission to their husbands is God's way of resolving _conflict_.

9. According to Proverbs 14:1, a woman can either _Build_ or _destroy_ her home.

10. I Peter 3:4 relates that a Christian wife should have a _Meek_ and _quiet_ spirit.

Questions for Thought
1. Why is it so hard in our society for a man to give and initiate love?
2. If you came from a home that was "maternally dominant" or "paternally dominant," how do you react to that home environment?
3. In terms of "rights and responsibilities" in marriage, do you think the greater pressure rests on the husband or the wife?
4. How are conflicts resolved in your home?
5. Are you raising your children as you were raised? How have you imitated your parents? How are you different?

2

What's Under the Hood?

Complexity of Relationships

In something as intimate as marriage our understanding of purpose and design is absolutely imperative. The goal of marriage is oneness. Genesis 2:25 states, "Therefore shall a man leave his father and his mother and shall cleave unto his wife, and they shall **be one flesh**."

This is very difficult.

Some people are good "lovers" but bad partners. Oneness must include the following dimensions: psychological, emotional, spiritual, mental, and physical. And as the two dissolve into one, there is a voluntary loss of identity. This concept should spread into the family. The family should be a unit. Tragically, in some homes, the family has become a filling station. Everyone comes into the house, fills up and leaves.

Even though statistics are many times meaningless, in this case they do say something. At the turn of the century the divorce rate was one out of every 37 marriages. Now, in the state of Michigan, the divorce rate is one out of every 2.6. There are many reasons for this, but it does illustrate the complexity of relationships. Courses are now taught on interpersonal relationships, group dynamics, and getting along with one another.

A beginning point in understanding the complexities of relationships is the Book of Genesis. Two principles set forth in Genesis 2:18 are (1.) we are lonely people, and (2.) we need other people. "And the Lord God said, It is not good that man should be alone. I will make him an help meet for him."

The first principle indicates that there is no such thing as a fulfilled spinster or bachelor. Please, no grumbling. I do not want to offend any of my single readers. Notice that I said "fulfilled." You can be happy. You can be secure. But all of us can relate to being lonely. Why did God make us capable of being lonely?

The spinster prayed, "Lord, give me a man, Lord, give me a man." Night after night she prayed, with no tangible results. Then one night an owl was perched on the limb outside her window. "Lord, give me a man," she prayed.

The owl responded, "Who! Who!"

"Just anyone, Lord, just anyone."

A unique chemistry known totally to God alone moves us toward relationships. The hope is that the loneliness will be eliminated.

I was involved in a program in Minneapolis, Minnesota, and as I was walking with a friend in the downtown section of the city, a man who had been drinking quite heavily was about half a block ahead of us. We were walking up a long hill and I said to my friend, "I hope that poor fellow makes it." Suddenly, the man fell straight backwards and banged his head on the sidewalk. Blood was flowing freely and we rushed him to the hospital. In a hospital room, after many stitches, we talked to him. Here indeed was a man who was extremely lonely. His family was broken, he had no friends, he was finding no help in the bottle—I do not think I have ever met anyone quite so lonely. Many of us seek relief through drink or drugs or something else, but it doesn't help.

The fact is your husband or wife represents flesh and blood. You cannot put a price on another person. That is why it is so tragic to see people who do not build bridges in their relationships. We should praise the Lord for our spouses, for having those special mates who care for us. The first psychological need the husband and wife meet is that of loneliness. Build bridges instead of walls.

Besides loneliness, Genesis 2:18 establishes the principle of complementing one another's needs. Couples work so hard to remake their spouses over into their images. What makes you so right? Maybe the struggle with your spouse is really exposing glaring weaknesses in you. In scores of counselling sessions I have seen this "remaking" principle. But there is no way that we can become the Holy Spirit. God means for us to accept others as individuals.

REAL "agape" love demands that you accept others and love them with their strengths and weaknesses. Very few people see that. Some people love "although" and some people love "because," but few people simply love. One of the greatest insights a couple can have is to see each other as individuals and be able to allow room for individuality instead of feeling their task is to remake or rebuild.

It's such a beautiful experience for a couple to ask, "Where do we complement one another? What do you do that I don't do? How can we be of help to one another?" Some people miss the whole point. When a wife tells her husband, "Don't touch me, get away from me," she is making a gigantic mistake. Or when the husband says, "I am not going to let you have the money," or some such nonsense, that too is an error.

I recall a counselling session with a doctor and his wife. The doctor's comments were, "I have been to graduate school, medical school and internship and all that goes into being a doctor, but when it comes to sex, there is a chemistry I do not understand." Whenever there was a difference of opinion in their home his wife would say, "No, you don't sleep with me, no sex, away...away." People use the complementing of needs as a wedge; be thankful for the needs you can meet in the beloved's life.

"Neither was the man created for the woman; but the woman for the man" (I Corinthians 11:9). But it also says in I Corinthians 7:2 that every man should have his own wife and every wife her own husband. There is a mutual base—a certain need that can be mutually met. I made the mistake in graduate school of telling my wife the results of a battery of tests on aptitude I took during a course called Psychological Testing. I scored in the two percentile in the mechanical area. This simply means that ninety-eight percent of the men tested are better mechanically than I am.

I told my wife, "If you want a light bulb replaced, I am not the one to do it. A leaky faucet? Don't ask me!" When it comes to the mechanical, plumbing, or building, go to my wife.

After returning from a recent trip I stood gazing in unbelief at the chess table my wife had made during my absence. The board was wood carved, multistained and she had also carved various chess pieces. Should this be a threat to me? Never! Unknowing persons might compare husbands with fathers, mothers with wives. The husband and wife who understand love and who understand the need to complement each other will beautifully grow together.

Let us explore four principles for better interpersonal relationships.

Principle No. 1: **God wants you to be a happy, peaceful person**. He is not the author of confusion, and He did not establish the home as an arena of argumentation. Psychologically, the inner man throbs for peace and freedom. If we have inner peace, with it comes quietness and softness. Irritations are not as apt to be interpreted as threats. Jesus Christ said in John 14:27, "Peace I leave with you, my peace I give unto you; not as the world giveth, give I unto you...." Also, there are no words to describe being inwardly released. Freedom is not defined by external environment or pressures; freedom is an inner escape. A person can be in an open field and be bound; another person can be in prison and be free. The thoughts of love, joy, peace and freedom imply that God wants us to be happy. Marriage can be the closest thing to heaven this side of heaven, or the closest thing to hell this side of hell.

The book in the Bible known as the Song of Solomon is sensual in the best sense. You have a few bold words like "breast" used in it, but obviously Solomon is striving to express an inner joy and happiness. You might do a word study on the words "love" and "beloved." The author says he loves his wife more than a herd of horses. Some of you women might take exception, but Solomon is seeking full expression in a cultural perspective. She was fun to be with and they enjoyed each other. God did not mean for a husband and wife to work out a complex schedule where they bump into one another on weekends. He wants you to be happy. **So be happy**. Enjoy one another.

When talking with a person who is bitter, upset, hostile or angry, the question should not be which side of a given argument is right. Both sides lose. They are both wrong. If your home is not happy, if it is characterized by hate, bitterness, hostitility—you all lose.

A woman came up to me after a seminar one night with tears running down her cheeks and said, "Duane, I can't tell you how the Lord has spoken to me tonight. Twelve years ago I got into an embittered argument with my father. I left the house and I have not been back. I have not seen him in twelve years." As we talked and shared, it became evident that it wasn't a question of whom had been right and wrong. For twelve years, this woman had no relationship with her father. She resolved that evening to go back to her father and hopefully see the relationship restored.

Principle No. 2: **Recognize where the pain lies**. It is amazing how quickly we react when we have an ache physically. But if it is psychological, we put it off.

I had a toothache once and when it started throbbing, I had no quandary as to what was the problem. I did not decide to wait for two or three weeks, or change my life-style, or do things differently. I wanted that tooth fixed—now! It was hurting! I wanted it pulled. So I went to a destist—who agreed—and out it came. I felt better. I'm not much for kissing dentists, but what a relief. I knew by the symptom, by the pain, that something was wrong. I went to the person who could fix it and he did.

There are many people who have lived with bitterness, anger, and hostility for years. You may have lived fifteen or twenty years with a marriage having these symptoms. And you know it. You have argued night after night, and you have harbored bitterness and hatred toward your parents, toward your spouse, toward your in-laws, and you have "hoped" that things would improve. I am convinced that God has had it in His mind to change the life-styles of many of you. But it cannot be done unless there is an honest confrontation with what the symptoms mean and a willingness on your part to change.

I don't ask much. I just want you to get a glimpse of yourself which is entirely different. There is a vast untapped resource within you that if even nudged will change your entire life. I Corinthians 2:9 reads, "But as it is written, Eye hath not seen, nor ear heard, neither have entered into the heart of man the things which God hath prepared for them that love Him." But with the potential a sensitivity to the symptoms has got to be developed.

Ephesians 4:31 states, "Let all bitterness and wrath and anger and clamor and evil speaking be put away from you...." But many Christians still deeply harbor bitterness and hostility. Do you love one another? Can you say that you love everyone in your extended family—the church? Do you love your

39

spouse and your children?

I recall the experience I had while in seminary during an intramural football game. Two of us preparing for the ministry came within an inch of getting into a fight on the football field. Very becoming of future preachers....We were in a class called interpersonal relationships where the professor told us that we would have to put our arms around everyone in the class and tell him that we loved him without any reservation. This was to be done before the end of the semester. I felt the other student was wrong. He felt the same way toward me. I put off the professor's assignment as long as I could. Finally, the confrontation took place. In great tenderness and love we said with sincerity, "I love you without any reservation." The concept of reconciliation means "closing the gap." Perhaps right now you know of someone you need to "love without any reservation." This entire book would be worthwhile if one of you would go to your estranged wife, husband, or teenagers and say it, and mean it.

A third principle: **be careful that you do not blame God**. I have had couples tell me, "We married outside of God's will." We hear such theological expressions as "God's perfect will" and "God's permissive will." So we start thinking that we were not in God's will when we married. Well, trying to blame the problems of a relationship on being outside of God's will is sheer nonsense. It happened. It's done. You are married. That is not to say that everything you did before you were married was part of God's perfect will or that mistakes were part of God's will. But the marriage has transpired and the mistakes have been made. Therefore, God wants you to start within that framework. One of Scripture's most meaningful psychological texts is Philippians 4:13: "...forgetting those things which are behind and reaching forth...." It is done.

We have Biblical passages that speak of the believing wife being able to help the unbelieving husband and vice versa (I Corinthians 7:14). The Bible relates that once the relationship is established you build upon it. But tragically, some people think, "I wish my husband were dead so I could be released." Incredible the way people try to cop out of relationships. "God, it's your fault. You should have stopped me from marrying this person." But we must remember that very often God wants irritations in our lives to be a means of refinement. What God may be trying to do with the points of tension in your relationship is to show you areas of your life that need improving. Perhaps your wife or husband or children can be your best teachers. God is trying to give you bases of empathy and understanding. He is trying to change **you**—let's make it simple. Often, we work so hard to change each other that we fail to realize that those areas of irritation are aimed by God at us.

Why not start believing that God wants you to take that marriage and try to make it all that it can become?

Logic might dictate our fourth principle. **Be willing to be reconciled**. Obviously, if you believe that God wants you to be happy, that symptoms do mean something, and that you should not blame your circumstances on God, then the final recourse is to be reconciled. In evangelical Christian circles, II Corinthians 5:17 is a very familiar verse. "Therefore if any man be in Christ he is a new creature; old things are passed away, behold all things are

41

become new." This is rightly viewed in the context of the Christian doctrine of salvation. But it is important to look at the verses which follow: "And all things are of God who has reconciled us to himself by Jesus Christ and has given us the ministry of reconciliation. To wit that God was in Christ **reconciling** the world unto Himself, and not imputing their trespasses to them, but committing unto us the word of **reconciliation**. Now then we are ambassadors for Christ as though God did beseech you by us. We pray for you in Christ's stead, be ye **reconciled** to God.''

The obvious theme here is reconciliation. As previously stated, reconciliation means "closing the gap." God wants us to close the gap that flaws the relationship. Where there is hostility and bitterness God wants that gap closed. He has given to us the **ministry** of reconciliation, the **word** of reconciliation. "Be ye reconciled to God." If you are violating God's principles, it is not a matter of your reaction to your husband or wife or children—it is God's standards which are being flouted.

Therefore, the starting point is reconciliation to God. We have to be sure that the right relationship is established between you and your creator. Any two people who really want to see a marriage be successful can do so if they are willing to move toward **adjustment** and **resolution**. Couples who come to me with a question or struggle are asked: "Do you really want to see the marriage improve? Do you want to see reconciliation?" If they are willing to do that then I can almost guarantee that the marriage has a chance for success. But if two people want to argue and bicker and are in a counselling session to use me as reinforcement to relate how wrong the other person is, very little can be established.

When I go into a home to talk with a couple, many times I will close with, "Well, I'm going to leave. But I am going to encourage you after I leave to wrap your arms around one another, look into each other's eyes and say, 'I Love you, I care for you.' " I smile and say, "I'm not going to look back in through the window, but I really encourage you to do it."

What am I saying? You have to **make a move**. You have to be willing to close the gap. If you do not get along with your spouse, if your house is a battlefield, if you cannot get along with your father or mother, God brought you to this point because He wants you to be reconciled. He wants you to say, "Father, I am sorry. Mother, I am sorry. My dear wife, I am sorry. My dear husband, I am sorry." See that gap close.

The prodigal son rehearsed a speech. After he left home, spent his money and ended up with the pigs, he said, "I will arise and go to my father and say...." He messed up a few words, but he did say, "I have sinned against heaven and before thee" (Luke 15:18).

Maybe many of us need to be reconciled.

Father, help it happen.

Questions—Test Yourself

1. According to Genesis 2:25, the ultimate goal of marriage is that two should become _One_ .

2. According to Genesis 2:18, two principles basic in marriage are: a) We are _lonely_ people, and that we _Need_ one another.

3. A good marriage will bring to both husband and wife a real sense of _Happiness_.

4. Neither was man _created_ for the woman, but the

43

woman for the man (I Corinthians 11:9).

5. The first of four principles shared in this chapter is that God wants you to be a _Happy_ person.

6. Finish this verse. Ephesians 4:31, "Let all _Bitterness_ and _Wrath_ and _Anger_ and anger and clamour and evil speaking be put away from you."

7. A third principle shared in this chapter is to be careful you don't _Blame God._.

8. Reconciliation means _Chosing the Gap._

9. The passage of Scripture dealing with reconciliation is found in _II Cor. 5:17-20_

10. The story of the _prodigal_ son found in Luke 15:18 is a good example of the proper understanding of reconciliation.

Questions for Thought

1. Why is it difficult for people to become "one flesh?" _Identity Problem   Bad partners_

2. Do you really feel you are fulfilled in your marriage? What areas have brought you fulfillment? What areas have not?

3. How do you and your husband complement one another in your marriage?

4. Are there special areas of "hurt," perhaps unresolved conflict or bitterness in your life, that have never been faced?

5. Are there certain people with whom you need to be reconciled? What makes you hesitate to take the first step?

3

Blowing Your Horn

Communication In Marriage

Three elements are necessary for a marriage to be successful: (1.) a proper understanding of agape love; (2.) comprehension of the proper roles of husbands and wives; and (3.) sound understanding of principles of communication.

Many of us open our mouths and assume that whatever flows is correct. When was the last time you thought, "I shouldn't have said that?" It is good to become conscious of the mistake, but we can take the logic further and learn from it. The tongue is an interesting instrument. It can express edification, love, warmth, or it can express bitterness, hate and hostility.

Communication, at its optimum, is the freedom to share any question, problem or thought with someone else. We build walls many times instead of bridges. How many people do you know with whom you can share any question, problem or thought? Some couples have been married ten or fifteen years and do not have the freedom to share any question, problem or thought.

The above definition was indeed calculated. The three key words are **freedom**, **share**, and **any**. **Freedom** connotes an intimate relationship and human relationships on any level are difficult to come by. We are apprehensive of face to face encounters because they demand exposure of idiosyncrasies and flaws. Thus, before there can be **sharing**, there must be an overcoming of our own identity crises. When we can accept ourselves and sincerely feel that God has not made a mistake with us, then there throbs an inner excitement in sharing what we are.

This speaks to the core of marriage relationships. When any thought, question, or problem can be **shared**, to God be the glory, you feel a sense of want and belonging that gives purpose to life.

Proper use of words can change your life. This chapter can change your life.

I want to present some principles that can change your whole concept of words.

Recognize that even a single word is powerful. "A word fitly spoken is like apples of gold in pictures of silver" (Proverbs 25:11). A word, one single word...I am not suggesting that we try to think through every single word we say. But the problem is that most of us react impulsively. We do not take the time to realize how we can hurt or help. I could make enemies very easily by saying something negative or critical.

My mother used to have her hair done every Friday. She would enter the house, fluffing her hair, and say "How do I look?"

"Mom, you look _____ " A word....

"Wonderful, terrific, great, terrible, horrible." The power was there to affect her attitude by one

46

word.

God meant for us to communicate. Proverbs 16:24 says, "Pleasant words are like honeycomb, sweet to the soul and health to the bones." We affect ourselves inwardly by what we say. We also affect others outwardly by what we say. "Sweet to the soul" refers to an inner dimension. "Health to the bones" seems to imply that God keeps our inner chemistry in a much better condition if we are not emotionally upset or critical.

The tongue carries in it the power of life and death. Proverbs 18:21 states this: "Death and life are in the power of the tongue: and they that love it shall eat the fruit thereof." I think of all the treaties that have been broken and of all the meetings in which world leaders have reached agreements. They all involve the same thing—words.

Obviously the antithesis of correctly used words is argument. Many Christian homes are filled with screaming, yelling and arguing. They are yelling because dinner is not on the table on time or junior is not moving fast enough.

Arguments could be constructive if we were objective enough to discuss how they could refine the relationship. But in large measure we are not. Therefore, they become destructive. They build walls; people argue over the same areas. Let me attempt to prove that to you. Suppose someone is telling you, "What a rotten, no-good you are...." Are you saying, "Yeah—that's right"? No, most of us are waiting to jump into the conversation to attack back, depending upon the freedom we have.

Therefore, unless you can have real objectivity, recognize that you are not going to change people's minds by argumentation. Just love them and do not try to become the Holy Spirit.

Let me offer five steps to successful argumentation, not so you can argue more intelligently, but so that the next time you are in an argument you will know exactly where you are. I hope these five steps will kill your next argument.

CONE OF ARGUMENTATION

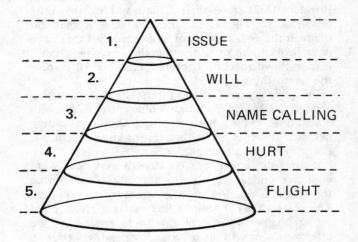

1. ISSUE
2. WILL
3. NAME CALLING
4. HURT
5. FLIGHT

The first step involves the issue. Obviously, before an argument can ensue a difference of opinion must exist. Any of us could sit down and in a short time find something on which we differ. You would think that rational, objective, Christian people could keep their differences of opinion on an issue level. Well, in case you have not realized it, many couples have difficulty here. And because people cannot resolve their differences at an issue level—or at least confine them to that level—they move to step two: will vs. will confrontation.

Whether you are talking about international conflicts or a dispute in a home, it all comes down to the quest for individuality—the desire to be sure your voice is heard. Most conflicts do not arise from a pretense of resolve, but from a pretense of argumentation. It is not unusual for will vs. will confrontations to produce an argumentative spirit. I have been in homes where three words could not be said without an argument. The people had developed that kind of spirit. One of the greatest joys of life comes in seeing argumentative spirits dissolved.

I remember one couple whose home I visited. They were literally throwing things at one another. These two people had come to the point of playing the will vs. will battle until their marriage was about to shatter. What a joy it was to leave that home three and a half hours later and see the husband and wife embracing. I cannot recreate the dynamics that changed that atmosphere, but one thing I do try to do is move those involved toward a base of resolution of conflict.

If no base of resolve can be found no agreement will be reached. The goal of marriage is oneness. Therefore, the interests of both must supercede the individual wills. Do you really want to resolve your differences?

Take any person with whom you have a conflict. Right now. Are you intelligent enough to see that it is a will vs. will conflict? Do you want to move that conflict toward a base of resolve?

The third step of "successful" argumentation involves name calling. Names like "stupid" and "dumb" crop up. Please note that now the argument becomes overt. It is now aggressive. These are occasions where fine, religious people have been known to swear. Shocking, isn't it? Why? Because pressure builds, hostility grows, and we fight or kick out unresolved conflict. And as noted...for what? If someone tells you you're dumb, then you just bring up the mother-in-law, and on into the night. Now we have moved from our base of resolve.

Step number four is what I call "hurt." This can be either physical or mental pain. I am amazed how many wives tell me they have been physically struck by their husbands. Why is it that a man will strike his wife or a wife will strike her husband?

It could evolve this way. In the course of a discussion (?) that is becoming hotter by the minute, the husband or wife comes to the conclusion that he or she is not able to put across his/her point. That person's thinking is "I'll shut him/her up." Physical pain follows. The assailant is trying to say, "I can't get you to agree with me, but I can make you stop arguing."

Most hurt is more subtle, however. When we come to the point where we deliberately want to hurt someone we want to make sure that it is equal to the pain that has been given to us.

Most couples are capable of instant pain. If your husband or wife is getting the best of you in an argument you can bring something from the past that you know will inflict pain. Maybe there was a mistake fifteen years ago. So to the surface it comes again.

The fifth step is flight or escape. Things come to the

point where you want to get away—the proverbial running home to mother or trekking to the local bar.

A pastor once called me and asked me to talk with a couple from his church who were having difficulties. When I arrived at this couple's home, the **husband** had his bags packed and was ready to go to his mother's.

A bit of reverse twist had occurred. We talked a couple hours and eventually he **did** go home to his mother. Notice the flight and escape patterns. Rather than resolve the problem he was running from it. Many people do.

Now with the five steps I have just enumerated you can determine exactly at what point you are in an argument. In fact, when it all begins you can say, "All right, we've left name calling, now let's move right down to hurt." Or you can say, "Let's move over to the will confrontation." Ridiculous, isn't it? So are most of your arguments.

Tragically, many of us go through arguments every day of our lives. Biblical principles with psychological perspectives exist, however, which can revolutionize such a miserable existence.

The first Biblical principle on communication that I would offer is: **if you have something to say, say it and be quiet**. "Let your communication be yea, yea: nay, nay: for whatsoever is more than these cometh of evil" (Matthew 5:37).

Many of us have spent hours and hours listening to the same things over and over again. Some teenagers have heard their parents say, "If I've told you once I've told you a thousand times...." And they have! Parents will expend hundreds of words to make the simple point that the garbage was not taken out or the bed was left unmade. The point

51

could be made with the simple words, "Take out the garbage." All of the extra editorial comments accomplish very little. Say what you have to say and be quiet.

Within this framework, **if we could only learn to respond softly**, what a difference it would make. "A soft answer turneth away wrath" (Proverbs 15:1). It involves the same issue—how to use words, how and when we say things. You might want to practice talking softly. Soft like pillow...soft like marshmallow.... Actually lower your voice and think light and so-o-o-ft. Move your voice to a lower case and leave it there. Now practice speaking that way.

Many of us by temperament are more prone to give harsh responses. Many of us can be turned off with such responses. It is not the words that are bothersome, but the way in which they are said. Learn to give soft answers and make soft comments. If someone asks us a question in an irritable voice many of us feel like responding in a similar fashion. What a challenge to respond softly.

We should learn to choose our words well. "He that hath knowledge spareth his words, and a man of understanding is of an excellent spirit. Even a fool, when he holds his peace, is counted wise" (Proverbs 17:27-28). By our ability to control our tempers, to choose words correctly and use them sparingly, we are showing the depth of our wisdom and understanding.

Another principle is that **we must be sensitive to communication cues**. Most of us have never learned the art of listening. If I suddenly started screaming at the top of my voice, "Fire, fire!" I guarantee that everyone within the sound of my voice would go into motion. But it is just as important to listen and take heed when your little one comes up to you and says, "Daddy, Daddy, look at my picture." Perhaps you cannot see where the trees stop and the water begins, but what your child is saying is that he or she wants praise and wants to be assured that it is a nice picture.

If I come home at night and my wife says, "Boy, have I had a hard day today," I have a number of options. I suppose that I might create some excitement by simply saying, "Doing what?"

"Doing what??!! I work all day, clean this house. What type of consideration do I get?"

I simply said, "Doing what?"

Or my response might be, "You think you had a hard day. Let me tell you about mine!"

She does not need to hear how lousy my day was. She is saying, "Help! Help! Help!"

Certain responsibilities come with being the spiritual leader of my home. One is that if I need strength at the same time she needs strength, it is my responsibility to give strength. It does not matter if the boss just fired me or if I got beat up five times on the way home, I am supposed to listen to my wife when she says, "Boy, have I had a hard day today!" My response should be, "Well, honey, let's go out to eat tonight," or "Why don't you relax and I'll take care of the kids for a while."

If you can simply begin listening to people, it can change your life. You must try to develop the ability to shove your own problems into the background and listen to the communication cues others will give to you.

Closely related is **the ability to use words that build up those around you**, as opposed to tearing them down.

"Let every one of us please his neighbor for good to edification" (Romans 15:2). Edification means building up. So, my role, when I meet someone, is to try to build him up both spiritually and psychologically. Think about how many words you use in a day that tear down. I try not to allow conversations in my home that tear down. We don't have "roast preacher" for Sunday dinner in my home. (I would need Alka-Seltzer for indigestion anyway!) I realize that if we criticize in a negative fashion this poisons our own outlook.

When you awake in the morning, say to yourself, "I'm going to spend the entire day saying good things. Anyone I meet will hear only cheerful and uplifting things coming from my lips."

I am now going to relate to you a principle that will change your life. You will never be the same. It will forever be embedded in your mind. Ready?

Be sensitive to the "pressure principle" of communication. Let me explain precisely what I mean. As two people are talking, a "pressure principle" is involved. There is a stress factor subconsciously active during communication. It moves from person to person; great strength lies with the individual who can consciously become sensitive to this and can objectively maneuver. Let me illustrate.

As people talk, they often do not listen to what the other person is saying because they are thinking about how they are going to respond. It is like a rubber ball being tossed back and forth between two people. If someone stops talking and looks at you, you are expected to start talking. You can "blow" someone's mind by saying nothing after he or she has made a remark that anticipates a comment. Or,

54

change the topic of the conversation. But as things usually go, it is like the rubber ball bouncing back and forth. Someone makes a comment, you make yours; he talks some more and then it is your turn again.

It is all subconscious. It is a life-changing principle if we can understand it. The reality of it did not come in a textbook—it hit me one day during the course of a conversation.

A public speaker can put pressure on an entire audience. The speaker can pause, look at the audience and say, "What do you think about this?" or "Isn't that correct?" From a secular perspective, Johnny Carson has mastered this. He will tell a "lousy" joke, pause and wait for his audience to "feel sorry for him and respond." The response is the important part.

I am not suggesting that we play games with each other, but that we grasp this principle and make it usable. The Lord Jesus Himself is the classic example. In the eighth chapter of John, Jesus is confronted with a woman who was caught in the act of adultery. The crowd is expecting Jesus to pass judgment on this woman. As you read the passage, you can sense the tension build as the pressure is placed on Christ. Notice what He does. He dismantles the whole crowd and puts the pressure back on them. He looks around the crowd and says, "The person without sin can throw the first stone." This is followed by awesome silence. The principle is in motion. The crowd is dispersed. Christ is aware of the pressure principle and He executes it by using only one sentence. The crowd leaves and Christ is alone with the woman. Think of the humor when Jesus asks, "Where are your accusers?"

There is no better application of the pressure principle than in the area of Christian witnessing. Christians need not be defensive about sharing their faith.

For instance, let's take the teenager walking down a school hallway with a Bible on top of his stack of books. Someone comes up and says, "What's that on top of your books?"

The teenager responds, "It's my Bible" (notice the pressure principle).

"What are you doing with a Bible at School?" he is asked.

The teen responds to the pressure by saying, "I'm a Christian."

"What's a Christian?"

"Well, I believe in the Nicene creed, the virgin birth...." and so on, the Christian teenager states.

The pressure principle has been used to put the Christian teen at a disadvantage. The Christian feels like some type of outcast and has been put in a defensive position.

But take the same situation over again.

The Christian teenager is going down the hallway and someone says, "What's that on top of your books?"

"It's a Bible, don't you have one?" the Christian teen responds.

"Well, yeah."

"Don't you ever read it?"

"Maybe once or twice," the Christian teen is told.

"Do you ever think about what the Bible has to say?" the Christian teenager quizzes.

"Not really," comes the response.

What has happened here? The initiative has been taken away from the inquirer. In our second example the Christian teenager has taken the pressure off himself and placed it squarely upon the other person. After all, the other person is the one who asked the question about the Bible. So why develop a defensive posture?

Finally: **be aware that you show the kind of person you are by the words you use.**

Two portions of Scripture worthy of study in depth here are James 3 and Proverbs 14-19.

James 3:10 says: "Out of the same mouth proceed blessing and cursing. My brother, these things ought not to be." Obviously, James is dealing with a problem with the church. It's incredible the way we are able to share a blessing one moment, but because someone irritates us, we suddenly find ourselves using words that are derogatory.

"The words of a man's mouth are as deep waters, and the wellspring of wisdom as a flowing brook" (Proverbs 18:4). This chapter of Proverbs goes on to talk about a fool's lips and what comes from them.

"A fool's lips enter into contention and his mouth calleth for strokes. A fool's mouth is his destruction, and his lips are the snare of his soul" (Proverbs 18:5-6).

"The words of a talebearer are as wounds, and they go down in the innermost parts of the belly" (Proverbs 18:8).

People reveal what they are inwardly by their use of words. John 7:38 tells of "rivers of living water" flowing from us. And James 3:17: "But the wisdom that is from above is first pure, then peaceable, gentle, and easy to be entreated, full of mercy and good fruits, without partiality, and without hypocrisy."

If you are thinking about taking your stand for the

Lord at work, or if you are going through struggles, remember that you reveal the shallowness or depth of your spiritual life by what comes from your mouth.

It would be an injustice to deal with principles of communication and not refer to breaking down interpersonal barriers. We all have people with whom we do not agree. One night during a conference a woman told me that she had not spoken to her father for twelve years. They had an argument, she left home, and it was twelve years before she returned.

We go about this all wrong. We assume that if we yell loudly enough, adroitly manipulate, refuse to talk for a while, or cry long enough we can reinstate the lines of communication. Instead, the walls may become higher and higher. Pretty soon it's possible for two people to bring up almost any topic and an argument ensues. How do you break down the barriers? How can communication that has been severed for years be reestablished?

Well, first realize that **with knowledge comes responsibility**. I have little knowledge in the area of auto mechanics. I would hope that when I have a problem with my car, a friend of mine who is knowledgeable in the area of auto mechanics will feel a responsibility to tell me what I need to do. With knowledge comes responsibility. And since you now have knowledge of the Biblical principles of communication you have some knowledge that another individual does not have. You also have the responsibility to share that knowledge. It's your turn to cross over into their world.

Secondly, **try to put yourself in the other person's shoes.** Do not try to scream or cry through the barrier—cross it! Paul said, "I become all things to all men that by some means I might win some" (I Corinthians 9:22). You have to cross into their world and perhaps for the first time in your life see things from their perspective. Paul said we should bear one another's burdens and thus fulfill the law of Christ (Galatians 6:2).

If you do not tear down that barrier, who is going to? We can never assume responsibility for others, only ourselves. Remember, with knowledge comes responsibility.

Finally, **live within the framework of the other person's interests**. Get your eyes off yourself long enough to ask, "What are his or her interests?"

Perhaps then you will see the beauty of Christian communication begin to unfold. What a joy to see barriers collapse. Some of you have never **communicated** with your spouse or children.

You've shared words with one another, but I trust that after this chapter, you'll have the freedom to share any question, problem or thought.

Questions - Test Yourself

1. Communication is the freedom to share any _question_
_____, _problem_ or _thought_ with someone.
2. Proverbs 5:11 states that a _word_ fitly spoken is like apples of gold in pictures of silver.
3. The five steps of an argument are:
   1) _issue_ — _different opinion_
   2) _will_ — _conflict — resolve_
   3) _name calling_ — _argumentation_
   4) _heat_ — _physical & mental_
   5) _flight_ — _escape_
4. Matthew 5:37 makes clear that if we have something to say, we should say it and _be quiet_.
5. Define a communication cue: _be sensitive_ _listening._

59

6.Being able to speak softly has to do primarily with the _____.

7. Edification is the process of *Building up.*

8. James 3:10 defends the principle that we are what we say by stating, "Out of the same mouth comes forth *blessing* and *cursing*. My brethren, these things should not be."

9. A *interpersonal* barrier develops when people refuse to resolve their differences and walls develop.

10. It is our fault if barriers are not torn down because with *knowledge* comes responsibility.

Questions for Thought

1. What is the pattern of communication in your home?

2. Why do we feel we cannot confide in most people?

3. How do we learn to communicate effectively?

4. How do most people build walls in relationships?

5. React to the thought, "With knowledge comes responsibility."

4

Checking the Oil

The Lubrication of Love

Of all our feelings, love is by far the hardest to define. And they say "love makes the world go around." I've told many couples that relationships can be established through three directions: sex, security and love.

Security and sex demand objects. Our society thrives on sex, and we can become a product of this. Complexes and insecurity many times dictate the need for a relationship. But...where do we learn to love?

If you face the facts of how your capacity to love was developed, you will find that there is a close relationship between your home background and the love you experienced there, and the feelings you express now. If you come from a home full of bitterness, hatred and anger, then it will probably be harder for you to love.

There must be an outlet, an expression. And tragically, when someone "uses" another person to meet his own needs, physical or psychological, he is revealing a lack of understanding of love. The challenge is extended to analyze yourself psychologically right now. Is it hard for you to love?

By contrast, however, the Bible tells us that "many waters cannot quench love, neither can the floods drown it" (Song of Solomon 8:7). Exciting, isn't it?

Regardless of whether we have been married one year or a hundred, we can all relate to problems and struggles. As we try to complement one another, conflicts and differences are going to arise. Whether it's heated waters or torrential floods, you will find that through it all love is the sustaining force. How you respond to crisis and how you respond to difficulties in interpersonal relationships indicate the depth of your understanding of love.

But you say, wait a minute! Two people don't get married if they don't love one another. I hate to jolt you, but surveys estimate that nine out of ten married people never experience love. Security and sexual bases are so overpowering in many relationships that the thing least experienced is love. Therefore, once the honeymoon is over and difficulties begin to arise—you start walking the floor with the baby, the dirty diapers and all of the rest—then you begin to recognize what is at the core of the relationship.

Let's meet head on the question of love. Am I in love? Can I, from an objective perspective, determine such?

Love strives to bring fulfillment to all of us. Psychology's "wheel theory" says that we all move toward the desire for fulfillment. We all have personality needs. These needs beautifully and warmly move us toward, "Haven't we met before?" Then there is self-realization; the chemistry grabs you. Finally, you find yourself searching for any

excuse to talk and be with her. The "tender trap" is
sprung. Do you relate?

"Wheel Theory"

Personality Needs

Fulfillment   Rapport

Self-Realization

Your needs have to some extent been fulfilled by
this particular individual. German philosopher and
theologian Franz Delitzsch, in his book **Christian
Psychology**, says that when God created man, he left
out a certain part of man's soul. And when God
created woman, he left out a certain part of her
spirit. Therefore, what man and woman try to do
subconsciously is to complement the needs of soul
and spirit. That leads to fulfillment.

All of you know deep down inside the quality of
your relationship. Every couple, if they are willing to
face it, knows the status of their relationship. We
can only bring into the marriage what we are. You
might be half of the problem. I have counselled
many people who work out a very elaborate
schedule. He bowls four nights, she is out with the
girls three nights, and they never see each other.
That tells more than we would like to admit. If on the
other hand there is love, you find real enjoyment
with your beloved. You look for every opportunity to
be with that person. The simple touch or spoken
word is appreciated.

Fulfillment involves the concept of oneness in a relationship. The ultimate of love is the voluntary loss of identity in the beloved. Sexual intercourse is and does symbolize oneness. It seems God meant it that way. If you read the book or saw the movie **Love Story** you know that it ends with the classic comment, "Love means never having to say you're sorry." Now, first don't get hung up on the words, "I'm sorry." The concept deals with an inner attitude. If in a relationship two people come to a base of oneness—if the love has achieved fulfillment—then the people involved do not have to drive each other to contrition. They don't want to bring each other to a point where they must be apologetic, or relate how sorry they are for what they have done. They already know they are sorry, and therefore the words do not have to be said. **It is** possible to establish a relationship that reaches this point. Thus, the goal is set.

Love is one of our eight feelings. The others are hate, anger, sorrow, fear, jealousy, joy and anxiety. All of these feelings are developed to different degrees in our lives. From the time we are born, it is as if we have eight little balloons with words like love, joy, anger and hate on them. As the maturation process evolves, certain balloons are blown into...others aren't. Therefore, it is easier for some people to laugh than others. As unbelievable as it sounds, some church people hate...even get angry once in a while. OHH...!

Consequently, if we choose to express love or to scream at our spouses, we should not be surprised if our children do likewise. Many times we find situations where Mom and Dad yell and scream at one another, and then the children pick up the

64

emotional tone and begin yelling. But Mom and Dad say, "Stop yelling!" Where on earth did the children learn that?"

We can learn much about our own emotional development by looking into our past. During a counselling session, a woman told me that when she was five years old, her mother, for a joke, tried to pretend that she had hung herself in the basement. The five-year-old was petrified. It was all a joke. Can you imagine the emotional strain and jolt that would be to a five-year-old? She went running out of the house and down the street screaming. We do not realize how emotions are developed.

We could take any one of our eight feelings and illustrate this. I remember when our Youth for Christ organization put on a program entitled "Scream in the Dark." The intent was to take the ingenuity of thirty-five college students "acting" as monsters, an old, dreary house, thousands of high school students expecting to be scared, and "brew" it all together. Step one was a maze to be crawled through and at the end of the maze was a chute. The kids were pushed into the chute and fell into the basement onto a pile of foam rubber.

One girl became aware that her friend, who had been in front of her in the maze, was now gone. She began groping in the dark, calling, "Mildred, Mildred, what did you do with Mildred?" Her girl friend was gone! "I am not moving another inch until you tell me what you did with Mildred!" Since she was slowing down the whole line of people in the maze, one of the helpers hidden by the maze decided to reach out and tap her on the shoulder. Can you imagine being on all fours crawling through a maze that is totally dark, and suddenly a hand comes out from nowhere and taps you on the shoulder? She almost set a new high jump record!

The guy said quietly, "Hey, if you stay to the left, you don't have to go down the chute." Now, that was a lie. There was only one place for her to go. She finally said, "All right, I don't want to go down that dumb chute." So she crawled ahead and down the chute she went. Then from the basement we heard, as she tried to crawl back up the chute, "You lied to me!"

As interesting as that might be, the purpose in part was to bring forth fear. Where did you learn to hate? We hate very easily. We laugh very easily. Somebody tells a lousy joke, and some of us laugh. For some of us, it takes some exceptional humor just to make us smile. We have all been raised in different emotional settings.

Our society develops men and women differently. What games do boys play? They play basketball, football, baseball, war, "Bang, bang, you're dead or I quit." At the age of six, a boy is expected to be a little man. He isn't supposed to kiss his father and if he picks up his sister's purse....It is built into fathers to have their boys be masculine.

Everyone can relate to the poor guy at school who appears to be something less than masculine. He is unmercifully ostracized. I recall a friend telling me about his young son playing in the yard. The boy next door called him over to the fence and said, "Todd, put your nose through the fence." Todd did and the boy next door bit his nose. Can you imagine standing there with your nose through the fence and having someone nibble on it? I asked my friend what his response was. He said, "I told Todd to slug him!" Boys have to be aggressive, independent and strong-willed to survive. What a tragedy!

Very early a "masculine mystique" is established for every young man. Tragically, the aggressiveness of this stereotype hurts his ability to understand love. Somehow being tender and compassionate are antithesis to football and "war." Thus, all fathers are concerned that their boys be able to compete and survive.

Girls have somewhat of an advantage emotionally. They play with dolls and their whole frame of reference is built around words like "tender" and "sweet." They are entitled to be mothers and show love in a special way.

I came home one evening and one of my little girls said, "Daddy, will you be my husband?"

"Have you talked to your mother about this?" I asked.

She answered that she had so I said, "Sure, I'll be your husband." We proceeded to go up to her room which was filled with her little furniture and she asked me to sit down. I thought to myself that there was no way I was going to get my feet under that tiny table. I sat down with my knees under my chin, and my little girl asked, "What would you like to eat?" I told her that I would like to have a steak. So she reached into "never-never land" and out of nowhere there appeared an imaginary steak. And she had potatoes and milk, too. If what she did was dumb, what I did was even "dumber." I picked up a knife and fork and ate it! She stood there waiting to be praised and emotions were developing, developing, developing.

So it is not unusual that by the time a boy or girl reaches high school it is easy for the boy particularly

67

to confuse love and sex. A guy will use love to get sex, and a girl will indirectly use sex to get love. They have grown in different directions and the maturation and conflict levels differ.

The responsibility of initiating love rests with the husband. Ephesians 5:28-29 says, "So ought men to love their wives as their own bodies. He that loveth his wife loveth himself. For no man ever hated his own flesh: but nourisheth and cherisheth it, even as the Lord the church."

Every man should ask himself what emotional pattern he is setting in the home.

There are different levels and degrees of love. Realizing that everyone has different emotional capacities, and that there is a correlation between the emotional environment and how emotions are developed, it is easy to see how one person is able to hate more and another to love more.

In American society, the word "love" has lost its meaning through overuse. We love school, we love chocolate ice cream, we love to work, we love our wives, we love our children. In large measure, the English language has rendered the word "love" meaningless. This is because we do not have other words to describe our many feelings, so we use love. Contrast the word "like" with "love." The difference is in intensity. It is not unusual for a teenager to say, "I like this person," or "I love that boy." As the relationship intensifies, the words subconsciously change.

The Greek language has three different words for love: eros, agape and phileo. "Phileo" is that kind of love that is fraternal. As I related in the chapter on "What's Under the Hood," when I was in a class in seminary, the professor said one day, "Fellows, if you can't love everyone in this classroom, you might as well forget about loving your congregation. Before this semester ends, I want you to go up to everyone in this class, put your arms around him, and say 'I love you without any reservation.' '' Well, frankly, there was a "friend" in class who had met me head-on in a football game one day and we had exchanged words. There was much reservation, but as the Lord worked in our lives during that semester, we came together one day and said to each other, "I love you without any reservation." There was none. But that is a fraternal love, phileo love, a love between brothers and sisters, the type often found in a family or a church.

As for the other two Greek words, eros and agape, it might be interesting to contrast the two. Eros refers to a lustful, predatory, self-centered love. Agape means, "I love you just as you are." They are extremely different:

Eros
1. Suddenly, without warning
2. Self-centered
3. One or more people
4. Compulsive need for reassurance
5. Characteristics, miss person
6. Sex: means to an end

Agape
1. Time and growth dimension
2. Other-centered
3. One person
4. Lasting trust
5. The whole person
6. Sex: conveys meaning

Eros love happens suddenly, without warning. Agape love has a time and growth dimension.

When I was a senior in college, I was walking across campus with a good friend. He suddenly stopped me in my tracks and said, "Who is that girl?" I replied that I did not know.

"Duane, I am going to marry her," he said.

"You don't even know that girl," I replied.

"I know, but I'm going to marry her."

This was in September and believe it or not, three months later during Christmas vacation they were married. They had all types of problems and struggles; the marriage hinged on the verge of collapse for years. There is great value in letting love take on a time and growth dimension.

People who do not really love each other can fear time. Insecure people rush into relationships. "I'd better make sure I marry her before she changes her mind." The Bible says that we should "love our neighbors as ourselves." Most of us do love ourselves. Love starts with self-acceptance.

In eros love, there is a compulsive need for reassurance. "Do you really love me? Will you love me when I am old and gray? What if I am in a car accident and handicapped for life? Will you still love me?"

In agape love, there is a satisfying trust.

Sometimes people think there is something mystical about the word "love." Teenagers are a shade more guilty. Let's put a young couple on a back road; they have just been involved in premarital sex and the girl says, "Tell me you love me." If that is what she wants to hear, that is what he will say. But in agape love, there is a trust. There is no room for jealousy in real agape love. There is an inner satisfying force. There is certainty in the relationship. You do not have to try to prove it in words, even though words are nice to hear. It is found in action and in that inner peace.

John 3:18 says, "Little children, let us not love with words or with tongue, but in deed and truth." The adage is, "Your life speaks so loud I can't hear a word you are saying." The translation for the word "walk" in the Bible is "action." An example is Galatians 5:16. "Walk in the Spirit, and ye shall not fulfill the lust of the flesh."

Eros love is self-centered; agape love is other-centered. Many people get married for what they can get out of the marriage, not for what they can give to the marriage. Men are probably more guilty of this than women. Do you really look out for your wife? As Solomon put it, are you "looking for ways to please your beloved?" The selfish tendency says "me first." Solomon pursues "ways" to create more fulfillment and happiness for his wife. Can you really say, "the banner over me is love?" (Song of Solomon 2:4).

Eros love involves more than one person. Agape love is centered on one person. Remember the beautiful vow you took, "For better or for worse, from this day forward until death do us part." It is all centered upon one person. In eros love, the person is still looking around.

A girl came to me one time and told me that she loved two fellows and she did not know which one she loved the most. What she really was telling me was that she did not love either one of them. In case you haven't noticed, many married people are still looking around. I have a trap question that I ask people who come in for counselling. Many times I will say, "What would you do if someone better came along?" Better? "Yes, better looking, more intelligent, better personality—whatever your concept of better is." Of course, the answer should be that there is no one better.

In eros love, people can fall in love with the characteristics and miss the person. In agape love, there is acceptance of the whole person.

Believe it or not, some spouses actually attempt to change one another! "If I could just get him away from his mother, or if I could just get her away from her father...."

And if you think that only teenagers fall in love with characteristics, you need to realize it is not true. On any age level we establish criteria for acceptance, both for ourselves and for the other person. These criteria probably reveal more about unresolved areas in our personality than they do about what we want in our prospective mate. How can we reach toward an "overflow" experience or a perfect love when we start with limitations? We hide behind walls and have few "tools" to tear them down. In some cases we have no desire to do so.

In eros love, sex is a means to an end; in agape love, sex even in the simplest form conveys meaning.

Sex to a person who does not really understand love is a means to an end. I do not know how many couples I have counselled where the husband will rush to a physical climax in sexual intercourse without having the ability to satisfy his wife or a desire to do so. Within the context of the Bible, this is referred to as defrauding (I Corinthians 7:5). If you use another person as a means to an end, then you are expressing sex and not love. With two people who really love each other, sex becomes a way of conveying meaning. Whether it's holding hands or sexual intercourse or something in between, both male and female sense meaning, fulfillment and love.

This chapter has basically dealt with an analysis of love as an emotion. Love, the desire for inner fulfillment, the basic root of interpersonal involvement, is so hard for many to understand and experience.

We want to give you three principles to make you a better lover.

Principle #1: **A direct correlation exists between your ability to love and your hang ups**. You must realize that love will only go to the wall of your complexes, and that is where it will be defined and interpreted. I John 4:18 states that "perfect love pushes aside fears...." Fears, complexes, apprehensions are all a part of your personal encounter with the feeling of love. Human relationships have to be an extension of you. "For now we see through a glass darkly, but then face to face. Now we know, even as we are known" (I Corinthians 13:12).

Many people are scared to death of face-to-face encounters. They are afraid of being known. They are afraid the other people might find out what they are really like. This keeps them from experiencing true love. Consider your shyness, your boldness, your loudness or any of your other qualities. Look at how they masquerade the real you.

To overcome fears, you must first face them. As much as possibile, identify them. Then comes the wonderful process. Any of us can be hypocrites until finally it becomes us. In other words, begin acting like you want to become. You must have a glimpse of the product and be that product. In time the acting will become actuality. The new you will be happening.

Principle #2: **To be a better lover, you must get your eyes off yourself and look at other people.** "Bear ye one another's burdens, and thus fulfill the law of Christ" (Galatians 6:2). The Book of Romans tells us that the law of Christ is that of love. Obviously, Christ shows us how to love. "God commendeth His love toward us in that while we were yet sinners, Christ died for us" (Romans 5:8). The best way for us to learn to love, even if our motives are entirely selfish, is to learn to look at someone else. Look at the needs around you. This is the way you learn to love. "If a man says he loves God and hates his brother, he is a liar" (I John 5:20).

While in college I heard the famous businessman J.C. Penny tell this moving story:

"In the inner city of Chicago, I parked my big car in front of a little store. When I came out of the store, a little ragged boy was walking around the car. He said to me, 'Mister, do you think I could go for a ride in that car?'

"I said, 'Sure, son, where would you like to go?'

"As he got into the car, the little boy said, 'Mister, can I ask you a question? Do you think I could take my little brother, too?'

"I thought, 'Sure enough, I've been had.' But I said, 'Yes, son, we can take your little brother, too.'

"So the little boy directed me down a back alley between decaying tenements, and he ran up a rickety flight of stairs behind the building. The next sight was almost beyond belief. Here came the six-year-old boy down four flights of stairs carrying a little crippled brother. As the little boy started down the stairs, I held my breath in fear they would both fall. I stepped out of the car and opened the door and finally this little boy, all out of breath, put his little crippled brother on the seat and said, 'Okay, mister, I'm ready for my ride.' ''

"He's not heavy, he's my brother," as the song goes. We learn to love by giving. Instead of fighting around your house over who has this chore or that, fight over the privilege of doing it. Instead of calling them chores, call them love—chances to show love to someone else. This is how to become a better lover.

Principle #3: **Learn to hurt with others**. "That I may know Him and the power of His resurrection, and the fellowship of His sufferings, being made conformable unto His death" (Philippians 3:10). You really begin to see what love is when you are willing to suffer with somebody. When someone else has a problem, you have a problem. When someone in your church is sick, you are "sick." The best way to learn to love is to give yourself to someone else and learn to identify with his hurts. The Lord brought this to my mind as I began to think back on my own marriage. In the early days of our marriage, if my wife had a problem, she had a problem—I didn't. "Take an aspirin, go to bed, you'll be all right." I really did not try to identify.

It's interesting how we can be convinced how right we are, but still be so very wrong. When working as an assistant pastor I was asked one day to call on a young man who was dying of cancer. I really did not want to go, but the pastor had asked, and so I reluctantly made the call. Yes, I counselled, I consoled, I even read a Bible passage and prayed. But as I was leaving he took my hand and said, "I guess you can really tell who has compassion when you get where I am, and see who cares enough to visit.''

Me? I went out to my car and wept. I knew.

"Greater love has no man than this, that a man lay down his life for his friends'' (John 15:13). This is precisely what God did through the person of Jesus Christ—in true love. He loved and He gave (John 3:16). May God help us to become better lovers.

Questions - Test Yourself

1. The four steps of the wheel theory are: _Personal Needs_, _Rapport_, _Self Realization_ and _Fulfilment_.

2. The ultimate of love in a relationship is _Loss own identity in the beloved_.

3. Our eight basic emotions are _Love_, _Hate_, _anger_, _fear_, _sorrow_, _joy_, _Jealousy_, _tenderness_.

4. Eros love is _self_ -centered, agape love is _Others_ -centered.

5. The Greek word of love that is fraternal (brotherly) is _Phileo_.

6. There is no room for _Jealousy_ in real agape love.

7. A direct correlation exists between your ability to love and your personal _Hang-up_.

8. To be a better lover you must get your eyes off yourself and _on others_.

9. Galatians 6:2 says, "Bear ye one another's _Burdens_ and thus fulfill the law of Christ.''

10. The ultimate of love is trying to learn to _Feel_ with others (Philippians 3:10).

Questions for Thought

1. Discuss the proportionate relationship of sex, security and love in your marriage. Which was the

hardest for you to experience?

2. Has your marriage brought you real fulfillment? Where do you still sense an emptiness and a vacuum in your relationship?

3. What was the emotional atmosphere of your home as you were being raised? Where did you learn to love?

4. Take the chart on eros and agape love given in this chapter. Break down the percentage of 16 points on each number. Example: Suddenly and without warning—10%, Time and growth dimension—6%. Do this to all six, add up the scores, and you will get some idea of how much of your marriage is eros, and how much agape love. Discuss.

5. Why is it so difficult for us to hurt with others?

5

Tuning the Engine

The Energy Source of Your Marriage

Man has struggled throughout most of his existence to understand himself. Is there a God? Is He really interested in me? Did He really create me? What is life? These universal queries consciously or subconsciously stagger us all.

I personally recall my struggles conceiving the essence of life. Does the spirit live on? Gordon Allport in his book **Becoming** states that there is a "propria," a life principle in each of us. This chapter will attempt to define this principle and equate it to marriage.

"And the Lord God formed man of the dust of the ground, and breathed into his nostrils the breath of life; and man became a living soul" (Genesis 2:7). In the drama of the creation account here is man, established in three parts: body (dust of the earth), soul, and spirit (breath of life). God, as master designer, created as no artist, no sculptor can. The artist draws men, the sculptor molds into a likeness, but it is **God** who created them.

There is that life principle—the human spirit. You

have a spirit...yes, you. It is not mysterious or mystical, but it does have a decisive function.

"And the very God of peace sanctify you wholly; and I pray God your whole spirit and soul and body be preserved blameless unto the coming of our Lord Jesus Christ" (I Thessalonians 5:23).

"For the word of God is quick, and powerful, and sharper than any two edged sword, piercing even to the dividing asunder of soul and spirit, and of the joints and marrow, and is a discerner of the thoughts and intents of the heart" (Hebrews 4:12).

When I was in high school I went to church one Sunday (that was a bit unusual at the time). It was my custom when I did go to arrive late and sit in the back. Usually I paid little attention to the services, but this particular Sunday the back seat was taken and the usher placed me in the third row. I was upset before the service even began. To make things worse, the pastor announced that the special speaker for the day was a missionary. It's not that he was old, but I was convinced that they must have dug him up that morning.

I was thinking in my adolescent mind, "Prunes have nothing over this fellow."

But if I live to be one hundred and ninety-seven, I will never forget Daddy Griggs.

The moment he arose he began to glow with excitement. He vibrated and bounced up and down. I thought to myself, how is it possible for anyone to get so excited about religion? Whenever he talked about his faith in Jesus Christ, he bounced double-time.

Looking at him from the third row, I thought: "This man claims to be a Christian and I claim to be a Christian. But what a contrast!" I sat there with my doubts, bitterness and hostility inside and watched Daddy Griggs. He was so excited he seemingly could not stand still. What was the difference?

God used that incident to launch me on a personal search. I saw that God had worked in this man's spirit in a very real, tangible and vibrant fashion. This missionary's human spirit was very much alive. It pulsated, drove and was highly motivated.

Daddy Griggs helped me grasp the meaning of the human spirit. Proverbs 20:27 states, "The spirit of man is the candle of the Lord, searching all the inward parts of the belly." Your spirit is your life principle, it is the candle of your life. I would define the human spirit as the furnace or energy source.

The spirit can be characterized. You can put a label on your spirit. The Bible talks about such things as a proud spirit or a haughty spirit. In I Peter 3:4 the wife is exhorted to have a "meek and quiet spirit." Indeed, the energy source inside of you has certain traits. That "spirit" dimension simply must be understood. The more we can understand ourselves and what we have to contribute to a relationship, the better the chances for success.

You do not ask certain people how they are because they will tell you. While attending seminary I pastored a small church. The first Sunday I was there I said to a lady, "Good morning. How are you?" She spent ten minutes responding. I cannot recall if she worked from the top-down or bottom-up, but every ache and pain was remembered. You talk about an "organ recital." I think she recited what was wrong with every organ!

Now, that was her spirit. What is your spirit like? If you were to characterize your spirit, what would it be? Are you a happy person, optimistic and loving?

Or are you critical, cynical, bitter and hateful?

You can begin to see how all this affects a marriage. What if someone with a tender and loving spirit has a mate who is bitter and cynical? Some of you have had an "argumentative spirit" for years. From the time you wake up until the time you sleep you are arguing. I counselled a couple who had argued for thirty-seven years. Imagine, thirty-seven years with little concept of how that could be changed. Think for a moment. How much arguing is in your home? Are you personally involved? Do you have that peace and meekness and quietness of spirit so you do not have to argue?

We should worship in spirit. "God is a Spirit, and they that worship him must worship him in spirit and in truth" (John 4:24). Two types of spirits are mentioned in this verse. When the word has a capital "S" it refers to God's Spirit, the Holy Spirit. A little "s" means the human spirit. It is possible to attend church and listen to the sermon and then be critical and negative at home, referring to the "dry" preacher. Perhaps, then, you are not worshipping, for you are to worship in spirit. The easiest way for you to turn your kids from the church is to have a negative spirit, and "roast" the pastor in their presence on the way home from church.

Focus on yourself. How do you worship? In spirit? David talks about a hunger and thirst after righteousness. As you sit in church and listen, a hunger and thirst after righteousness should grow within you. Just as a little baby naturally reaches out for milk, the hunger and thirst in our spirits should cry out, "Teach me! I want to learn!"

A church with people like this will affect the spirit that exists in the pulpit. Let it start with you.

Bitterness and hateful attitudes can cut into our spirits. As a result, many people in church on Sundays are not there in spirit. You end up with numbers of people in church who are not really worshipping.

My father used to work midnights and come to church Sunday mornings straight from work. Now to his credit, he was tired but he was there. He had quite an ability to launch into an extended prayer just as the minister said, "Open your Bibles...." But it was not the praying that was bad—it was the snoring that accompanied it!

It's been said that if you took all the people who fall asleep in church and laid them end to end they would be much more comfortable! But regardless of how long the minister preached, the minute the last "Amen" was spoken, my father was awake.

Now I love my father very much, but the truth is that when he was in church he was not there in spirit. In fact, he was barely there in body!

An honest evaluation of our churches would reveal that relatively few people worship in spirit. Yet the New Testament speaks of Christians whose spirits burned within them. How we need to recapture this!

Our football coach in college always admonished us in the locker room during halftime, "Do better! Hit 'em harder—Go get 'em!" He was not appealing to our physical ability. There was no way in a ten-minute speech he was going to make us physically better. He was aiming his speech at our spirits, trying to get us highly motivated with a sense of urgency, direction or confidence.

That's you. Get fired up! Get motivated! Your marriage CAN succeed! Let me appeal to your spirit. Those struggles can be resolved. You can be different.

Unresolved conflict in your life affects the spirit dimension. Notice that I'm talking about unresolved conflict. As most of us get older, our parents seem to get smarter. I recall walking the floor with our first daughter about three o'clock one morning. I thought, "I wonder how many times my parents walked the floor or stayed up late with me?" If the conflicts are understood, at least in part, then the bitterness and hostility can be modified. Pressures and tension can bring forth conflict.

Some parents, however, take their bitterness and hostility out on the child. The child is spanked three times harder than he or she deserves because the mother subconsciously thinks, "That's for my mother." In a moment of rage the man strikes his wife and subconsciously says, "That's for the time my dad used his belt across my back."

A girl came to me one day and told me how much she hated her mother. Time and time again in the conversation I heard, "I hate my mother...I hate her."

She convinced me. Finally, I looked at her and said, "Do you know the difference between hate and sympathy?"

"Yes," she answered.

"Wouldn't it be far better to feel sorry for your mother than to hate her? That hate seems to have gotten control of you."

If you have hostility toward friends, relatives, parents, spouse or children, then unresolved conflict lies within your spirit.

A factor related to this involves will-versus-will struggles. Rivalry situations between siblings or struggles between husbands and wives illustrate

84

this. One boy told me he could always tell when his parents had a disagreement because his father would emerge from the bedroom, blanket and pillow in hand, headed for the couch.

Adults play an interesting game in their will-against-will struggles. The mate is hurt and subconsciously says, "All right, if he does that, then I will do this." That is in turn countered on the other side with a similar stubborn response. It reaches the point where one of them says, "You're not going to get your way," or "I'm going to hurt you just as much as I can." Whether the "punishment" involves inflicting physical pain or withholding sexual relations, the intent is the same.

Are you harboring a will-against-will conflict? If so, your spirit is wrong.

Conflicts sometimes arise as a result of faulty family background. Some people come from families where they are encouraged to psychologically "act out" their feelings. One school of thought prevalent today defends this, even though it often results in overt hostility and animosity. Also, in such atmospheres the effect on the spirit is often not taken into consideration. When a person who all of his life has "acted out" his feelings marries someone who has a meek and quiet spirit, conflict and frustration arise. For example, if a man comes out of a ghetto background of hostility and marries a girl from a decisively Christian background who is very structured in her thinking, there is a high potential for trouble.

"Fine, Duane," you say. "How do I get a better spirit in my home?"

First—and certainly the most basic point—**realize your spirit can change**. Let me repeat. It can change.

There must be self-realization as to the spirit and a willingness to change. Without these components, the principle is impossible.

If you are bitter, hateful and resentful; if you have unresolved conflict within; if you come from a home where open hostility occurs—then, praise God, your spirit can be changed!

Psalm 51:10 states the outcry of David, "Renew a right spirit within me." In the original text, the word "renew" connotes "better than new." Can you imagine something "better than new?" Suppose you buy a brand-new car, park it in front of your house, peek through the window and imagine it "better than new." The implication obviously is that for change to occur we must "retreat before existence." If not in reality, in concept we must get a glimpse of starting over again. Praise God! Any day can be a "new beginning."

"Renew a right spirit within me." There must be a throbbing desire to have a new marriage at any cost. How must I change? Take a moment and analyze the argumentative spirit between you, your spouse and siblings.

There is no way to become an instant psychologist and have concise understanding of a will-against-will struggle. But you are intelligent and you know whether something is missing in your marriage. You know whether your marriage is as it should be.

This leads us to a second principle. **Our hangups and our fears unmask unresolved problems in our marriages**. God has not given to us a spirit of bondage.

"God has not given us a spirit of fear, but of power and love and of a sound mind" (II Timothy 1:7).

If we have fears and hangups—if we are

86

bound—then something is wrong in our spirits. If we cannot talk to our spouses, or if a communication problem has developed between us and our teenagers, then something is wrong in our spirits. God has not given us a spirit of fear. If we are in bondage then we need to understand how to break out and be changed.

It may seem naive to say it, but indeed shout it loudly: **You do not have to be in prison to be in bondage**! There are many free people walking the streets who are bound people. For that matter, there are some in prison who are free. Christ said, "You shall know the truth and the truth shall make you free" (John 8:32). Truth releases. As understanding comes, chains drop. This is a fact on any level, whether it be social or intellectual. In counselling, what a joy to see a couple experience this self-realization. Nothing is more enjoyable than seeing walls collapse. I think of a father and son who went camping together for the first time when the boy was seventeen. After two weeks together they finally realized they were relatives. What a joy!

Thirdly, **understand the dynamics within the spirit when salvation occurs**. Few understand the reality of having that beautiful marriage of God's Spirit and their spirits. Certainly it takes deeper meaning when both husband and wife sense within them the Holy Spirit. Theological expression must become personal reality.

Romans 8:9 states, "If any man have not the Spirit of Christ he is none of his." When the repentant heart reaches to a redeeming God, among the attributes of this grace is the personal indwelling of the Holy Spirit within man's spirit. We can sense, yes, some fear the term, but we can feel Him within.

John 3:6, "That which is born of the flesh is flesh, but that which is born of the Spirit is spirit." (Remember, capital "S" Spirit denotes God's Holy Spirit. Little "s" spirit denotes the human spirit.) This is part of what is called conversion. Man is changed (II Corinthians 5:17). Man is changed by God.

As the Holy Spirit "nestles down" with our spirits an interesting process begins. Man was created, you see, with three basic parts: spirit, soul and body. I Thessalonians 5:23, "...and I pray God your whole **spirit**, **soul** and **body** be preserved blameless...." I hope that you can sense the dynamics of God's Spirit within your spirit—your furnace—the energy source. God, however, wants to fill us all. He wants to **fill** us with the Spirit. Thus, the growth process ensues. As heat goes through the ducts to warm the house, so His Spirit wants to fill all your soul and body.

There might be "parts" of our souls or bodies we do not want to be filled. "Not my emotions, Lord, not my drives, Lord," we say. Since we have wills, we can submit or resist. But of course, the Scripture states, "Be not deceived. God is not mocked. Whatsoever a man soweth that shall he also reap" (Galatians 6:7).

We are fooling only ourselves. He wants us to open the doors. He wants us to say. "Yes, my conscience, Lord, take my memory, please, my appearance, what a joy to give you my senses, my instincts." He wants all. Because He is selfish? No, such is not an attribute of God. As we grow we live...as we grow we live...as we grow we live. God wants the fruits of our spirits to be love, joy, peace, longsuffering, gentleness, goodness, faith, meekness, self-control

88

(Galatians 5:22-23).

Know what? Eventually you will sense God's Holy Spirit flowing through you. In John 7:37-39, Christ related to the Pharisees, "If any man thirsts, let him come unto me and drink. He that believeth on me, as the scripture hath said, out of his belly shall flow rivers of living water. But this spake he of the Spirit, which they that believe on him should receive: for the Holy Ghost was not yet given; because that Jesus was not yet glorified." The Pharisees did not understand; few do today. God's Holy Spirit can flow through you. Personally, I believe as the doors open and man senses the flow of the Holy Spirit, yes, the "filling of the Holy Spirit," he grows.

The spirit is a crucial dimension of personality. Analyze your spirit. Reflect on the "spirit" in your home. Have you sensed the encounter of your spirit and God's Spirit? What a joy, what a thrill to relate **YOU** can be changed!

Questions - Test Yourself
1. The human spirit is best defined as _____ *Life principle P. 79*.
2. According to Genesis 2:7, man is a trichotomy, (three parts), namely: *Body*, *Soul* and *Spirit P-79*
3. Passages like I Peter 3:4 which speak of a meek and quiet spirit give to us the principle that our spirits can be *Changed Characterized P-81*
4. God is a Spirit, and they that worship Him must worship Him in *Spirit* and in *Truth* (John 14:4).
5. Unresolved *Conflicts* in your life affect the spirit dimension. *P-84*
6. The first principle in establishing a better spirit in your home is realizing the human spirit can *Change P-85*.
7. Psalm 51:10 states, "Renew a *Right* spirit within me." *P-86*

8. Our _Hangups_ and our _fears_ p-86 unmask unresolved problems in our marriages.
9. It is exciting to realize that if we know the truth, the truth can make us _Free_ (John 8:32).
10. According to Galatians 5:22-23, four fruits of our spirits that God desires are: _Love_ _Joy_ _Meekness_ _self-Control_ p-88

Questions for Thought
1. If you were to characterize your spirit, what word would you use and why?
2. Why are most people unable to worship in spirit?
3. Can you relate how unresolved conflict and pent-up hostility has affected your marriage?
4. Have you sensed a change in your spirit since your encounter with the Lord?
5. React to the statement: "Our hangups and our fears unmask unresolved conflict in our lives."

6

Avoiding Collisions

Will Vs. Will Confrontation

Why should the question of the will be considered in a book on family life?

Well...the answer is quite simple. Probably not a day goes by but that your will comes into conflict with someone else's.

"Honey, would you take out the garbage?"

"Dad, would you help me fix my bike?"

"Dear, would you fix this tear in my trousers?"

Have you ever gotten into an argument with your husband or wife? Have you ever had children who squabbled? Unless your home is a whole lot different from most, these things occur. The only way there can be any hope of stopping this pattern is to come to grips with the reason God gave you a will.

I recall one evening in our home when my wife had fixed a very delightful chicken casserole and our second little girl decided she was not going to eat. She had eaten this dish many times before, but she had made up her mind not to eat it that night.

I questioned her, "Tami, are you feeling all right?"

"Yes," she replied.

"You're not sick?" I queried.

"No," she said.

"Tami, please understand that you are expected to eat your dinner. Is that clear?"

"Yes."

But still no response as far as eating the casserole. So I began the diplomatic approach.

"Tami, you don't want to see your mother cry, do you? After all, she has worked hours on this casserole."

That did not seem to affect her. So I became more desperate.

"Tami, if you don't eat your supper, your father will spank you." No response. So I warned her again.

"Tami, if you don't eat this casserole your father will spank you. Is that clear?" I said.

"Yes."

"Are you going to eat it?"

"No."

To make a long story short, she was spanked once and still would not eat the casserole. She was spanked again and about then I got a look from my wife that seemed to say, "Are you sure you know what you are doing?" My return look assured her that I was doing the best I could.

Finally, I looked at Tami and said, "Tami, open your mouth." She opened her mouth and I said, "Tami, keep your mouth open." I proceeded to pick out the best piece of chicken casserole I could find and put that piece of chicken right on her tongue.

I said, "Tami, close your mouth." She closed her mouth. "Tami, chew the food." She chewed the food. "Tami, swallow the food." She swallowed the food. And I looked at Tami and said, "Tami, that wasn't bad, was it?''

She shook her head no and sat down to eat the rest of her supper.

I must confess that this was at best a calculated risk. The issue was not whether or not my daughter ate her food. The issue was that at the ripe old age of four, she had decided to bring her will to bear, and suddenly we had a father-versus-daughter will confrontation.

What is the will really like? You can be strong-willed or naive. Many people are stubborn, independent, or strong-willed and never stop to think what effect this has on a marriage. Why do arguments occur? Why is there constant confrontation between husband and wife or among teenagers? It is because of the will dimension. Each of us has inherited the idea that we have to protect anything that is part of our acquisitive instinct. In other words, anything that belongs to us.

Many of us do not realize that when we yell and scream at our children we are making them strong-willed. Ask yourself a few questions. How much do we argue around the house? Do I have equal feelings toward everyone in my home? Am I more closely drawn to one child (or parent) than to another? If so, why? Which parent is more strong-willed? What issues do my spouse and I bring up over and over again?

If you are able to analyze these questions you will see that many times adults and children argue over the same things without realizing what this says as far as the will is concerned. God gave each person a will as part of the personality. But God wants the Christian to give that will back to Him. I repeat: give the will back to Him.

The bigger issues that this country faces also involve the question of the will. A teenager came up to me one night after a meeting in Plymouth, Michigan. This was during the time of the Vietnam War and he asked me what I thought of the war. How was I going to field that question in a group setting?

I looked at him and said, "Do you know why there is a war in Vietnam?"

"No."

"Do you love everyone?" I asked.

"No, I can't stand my old lady," he responded.

I answered, "That's why we are in Vietnam. If people can't get along on a one-to-one relationship, should there be any great surprise that countries can't get along?"

Do you love everyone? A question such as this brings things closer to home than Vietnam, racial tension, or any other social issue. Is your home filled with arguments and constant conflict over the same issues?

You must realize why your will is there. Otherwise, you will go to your dying day arguing with your husband or wife and wondering why your children do not care to be around you.

Remember the woman I referred to who walked out of her father's house after an argument with him and did not return for twelve years?

Many people do not want to resolve their differences. Their wills become so established and they become so set in their own ways that any communication moves in only one direction. "You listen to **ME**. Listen to what **I** have to say." We need to realize that the problems we find in most of our homes today center on the matter of the human will.

In the Bible, James chapter four gives a step-by-step breakdown of how God changes the will. It will do wonders for your attitude toward your family if you can recognize what God wants you to do with your will. In my judgment, these seventeen verses move in a progression (one step at a time). The climax is that God wants you to give your will back to Him. But some have never taken the first step. So get on your walking shoes...we're going up the steps.

The **first** step...you must **recognize the inadequacy of the HUMAN WILL** (James 4:1-5).

"From whence come wars and fightings amonst you? come they not hence, even of your lusts that war in your members? Ye lust and have not; ye kill, and desire to have, and cannot obtain: ye fight and war, yet ye have not, because ye ask not. Ye ask, and receive not, because ye ask amiss, that ye may consume it upon your lusts. Ye adulterers and adulteresses, know ye not that the friendship of the world is enmity with God? whosoever therefore will be a friend of the world is the enemy of God. Do ye think that the scripture saith in vain, The spirit that dwelleth in us lusteth to envy?"

The word "member" refers to our different parts as persons. We are told in I Thessalonians 5:23, "And the very God of peace sanctify you wholly, and I pray God your whole **spirit** and **soul** and **body** be preserved blameless unto the coming of our Lord Jesus Christ." Notice the three basic "members," or parts—spirit, soul and body. This concept is reinforced in Philippians 2:7 and Hebrews 4:12. Emotions, intellect, memory and the will are among our "members." It is the will that creates the wars and fightings among our members. It is the will that

95

strikes back. It is the will that activates anger, bitterness, and hate. By definition, these members take on interpersonal dimensions. "You lust, you kill, you desire to have, you cannot attain." That takes in the whole dimension of will.

"Who does he think he is pushing me around? I'm not going to let my children talk to me that way." If you have ever thought this way, that is your will.

If you can recognize the dynamics of what has happened to your will, that perception can lead you to recognize the inadequacy of the human will.

When I was little my mother used to spank me (I'm sure deservedly so). After a while she would come up to me to kiss me and make up.

My response was, "Get away from me." My hands would shoot over my face. "I don't want you to kiss me." You've hurt me; so I will hurt you.

It seems such frustrations should connote we need Someone more than ourselves.

On up the stairs. Step 2, you must **understand humility**. James 4:6,10: "But he giveth more grace. Wherefore he said, God resisteth the proud but giveth grace unto the humble. Humble yourselves in the sight of the Lord, and He shall lift you up."

Some are more adapted to understand humility than others. People who need help in marriage generally are strong-willed individuals.

Humility is recognizing what we are in relationship to what God is. In our society we feel we cannot trust anyone. Get them before they get you. We build walls around ourselves. Maybe it is wise to take a man for what he claims to be. The thrust of the proof rests on him. Why should we become negative and critical?

By way of contrast, let's look at what preceded the

crucifixion of Christ. In the upper room, Jesus got down on his knees and washed the feet of his disciples. This was not a famous athlete, the president of a bank or a professional businessman. This was the Son of God. This was God Himself in human form.

"Being found in fashion as a man, he humbled himself and became obedient unto death, even the death of the cross" (Philippians 2:8).

When Peter refused to have Christ lower himself to wash his feet, Christ responded to Peter, "I do this for an example" (Matthew 13:15).

Many of us have never come to the point of realizing what we are in relationship to what God is. Verse 6 states, "God resists the proud but gives more grace to the humble."

Now my friend, if you accept the premise that God above has a vested interest and is concerned about you, you want to crowd up close to Him. Do not antagonize. Therefore, if we are to understand God's unmerited favor—His grace—in our homes, in our personal lives or in our ministries, we must understand and practice humility. Have you recognized what you are in relationship to what God is?

Now on up the steps. Step 3, you must **submit to God**. James 4:7: "Submit yourselves therefore to God, resist the devil, and he will flee from you."

It is this verse that puts the whole chapter into focus. If I Corinthians 13 is the love chapter and Hebrews 12 is the faith chapter, then it is this verse that makes James 4 the will chapter.

The words "resist" and "submit" definitely characterize our wills. If I ask you to do something for me you have two options. You can say yes and

97

submit to my will or you can say no and resist. That is true in your home, too. Confrontations in most homes are built around arguments back and forth; i.e., making the bed, taking out the garbage, or raking the leaves. We can tell a great deal about ourselves from these two words—submit and resist. Do you find yourself cheerfully and gladly submitting? Or do you find yourself resisting, arguing and bickering?

"Submit yourself therefore to God, resist the devil and He will flee from you." God and Satan are antithesis. If I want the blessings of God in my life I have to pattern my life by the principles and rules he has given to me. If I give myself to the activities of this world, then in fact I am following the principles of the prince of this world—Satan.

"Resist and he will flee." A truly profound promise. I believe we resist Satan by recognizing temptation before it conceives, and then refusing to yield to such. It is the temptation that leads to lust and to sin and to death (James 1:13-15). If you choose not to heed God's will, not to have fellowship with God's people, then that is your option. But never forget Galatians 6:7. "Be not deceived, God is not mocked. Whatsoever a man soweth, that shall he also reap." One fear I have, and basically only one—being out of the will of God. I am aware that God can push pretty hard if I choose to resist Him. Even as I was writing these words, a girl related to me that she was rejecting God and giving herself to the occult, drugs, sex, and alcohol. Notice that she had made her choice. Joshua 24:15, "Choose ye this day whom ye will serve."

What is your will like? To whom do you submit, Satan or God?

Step 4, you must be **clean**. James 4:8, "Draw nigh unto God and He will draw nigh unto you. Cleanse your hands, ye sinners, and purify your hearts, ye double minded." God wants you to realize the inadequacy of your will and what it means to be humble. He wants you to be careful to whom you submit. He also wants you to be clean—that is an act of the will, too.

Our society thrives in the name of freedom on filth. Satan has taken so much that God meant to be good (James 1:17) and made it dirty. We are the product of our total environment. Thus, as we give ourselves to these activities, we become soiled and spotted (James 1:29).

Recently I counselled a high school girl at a church retreat. She went to church, appeared to live by all of God's rules, was secretary of the church youth group, and at that retreat played the piano. But she said, "Duane, I want to tell you what I am really like and what I am really doing." She told me that about every other weekend she would go to her sister's house. Her sister was not a Christian. From Friday night to Sunday afternoon this apparently fine Christian girl would live like the devil with her sister. When the girl would return home on Sundays, she would tell her mother how she and her sister had shared "spiritual truths."

With tears flowing down her cheeks she wept, "What a phoney I've been. Will God ever forgive me?"

Now not only was this gross hypocrisy, but it also says that this girl saw very little meaning in being a clean vessel. We rob ourselves. And it is hard for many of us to get insights into the world and how television, violence, movies and magazines have

99

subconsciously affected us.

To me, as a psychologist, it is ironic that the verse says, "Cleanse your hands and purify your hearts." Two steps are involved.

A tribe in Africa has a very interesting custom. If a man is caught in adultery, the practice is to cut off his right hand. Shocking isn't it? If he is caught again in adultery, they cut off his left hand. Of course, most men in that tribe who are caught in adultery lose only one hand, but can you imagine that kind of law in this country? However, looking at this verse practically, we must admit that we would have a difficult time in our sex lives if we did not have hands. God knew what he was doing when He said, "Cleanse your hands." For we find that our senses get us into a good deal of trouble. This applies not only to our overt acts, but also inwardly because our hearts must be purified. No greater challenge exists than to come to a realization of what the world is, how the world has affected you, what has happened to you inwardly, and then to develop that perception inwardly to the point where the temptation is minimal and you are clean inside. God wants you to be clean.

On up the staircase. Step 5, you must **be broken**. "Be afflicted and mourn and weep: Let your laughter be turned into mourning and your joy to heaviness" (James 4:9).

Why doesn't everything go right? Why do the valleys accompany the mountaintops? Why? Because most of us, like Peter, have to go through the breaking process. Before many of us can be usable, our wills have to be modified. I spent a part of my life on the streets of Detroit. There it was a matter of will against will, or who was the strongest, fought the hardest or was the most aggressive. I did not know what tears were. I did not know what it meant to be so concerned about someone else that I could cry. I considered crying a sign of weakness. But God was right and I was wrong. Before I began to be usable, God had to take me through a breaking process. Perhaps your marriage went through a great deal of heartache and agony before it began to stabilize. Or perhaps you know heartache as it concerns your children. David begins the 51st Psalm by saying, "Have mercy on me, O Lord." He was aware that he had gone through a breaking process.

One of the most sobering experiences in my life occurred while driving home from college. After a full day of activity, there was an emergency phone call and I left to make the two hundred mile drive to Detroit. After driving most of the night, I fell asleep at the wheel, and rolled the car down a hill. The car was completely demolished. The windows were shattered and the roof was pressed against the steering wheel. But by the grace of God, the only injury to me was a small cut on my nose from the glass.

God had a purpose in that experience. As the car was rolling over and over I was convinced that I was going to die, that it was all over for me. But this was part of God's design to bring me to the point where I could see what my will really was.

And in my home, just as in yours, I had to learn most of this the hard way. God wants you to be broken. Perhaps God has you reading this book to make you aware that you are strong-willed, and that you will not be able to be used by Him until you realize why there has been affliction, mourning and weeping in your life. Many of you have turned against God and said, "If there really was a God, why would this happen to me?" On the contrary, God has shown His grace to you by trying to make you usable.

Step 6, you must **view people differently**. When you are truly broken, when your will is finally changed, you will see people in a much different light.

"Speak not evil one of another; he that speaketh evil of his brother and judgeth his brother speaketh evil of the law and judgeth the law" (James 4:11).

I had a very difficult time seeing how this verse fit. But when it hits you, it's a grabber. Do you talk about people...your neighbors? After you go through a breaking process you will begin to see your wife, your children and your loved ones from a much different perspective. You will find that those walls built up over the years begin to come down. You will find that you are not trying to tear people down, or trying to find people to reinforce you in how terrible you think your spouse is. Instead you will find you are moving toward a deeper and more meaningful relationship.

God, you see, wants to change your tongue. Tied right on to your tongue is your will. When you are broken, you become more usable.

One of the most blessed counselling sessions speaks to this. It involved a strained father-son relationship. The father was resistant from the beginning. He sat there with a very defiant look on his face. He made it clear that he wanted no part of the counselling process. His son had quit school, he was very heavily into drugs and was about to ruin his life. His father seemed to feel no sense of responsibility. I talked to the parents and had three sessions with the son. The father and son rarely talked. For a number of weeks the father had wanted the son to paint the garage, but the son had resisted. One day when his father was away the son decided to surprise his father and paint the garage. The father returned home while the son was still painting and began to criticize the young man's work. The son picked up the paint can and threw it at his father. He jumped onto his motorcycle and was gone for five days. The father was obviously irate. He did not realize that in part he had caused that paint to be thrown at him.

After the three sessions with the son I met with the parents. After an hour, I told the father, "In a few minutes your son is going to walk into my office. I encourage you to go up to him, put your hands on his shoulders, and say, 'Son, I'm sorry. I have made many mistakes. Will you please forgive? I want to be a better father.' " That was totally out of character for this strong-willed, belligerent man who had made a strong-willed, belligerent son.

The son came shuffling in. The father walked over to him, put his hands on his shoulders and said, "Son, I'm sorry. I have been a poor father. Will you ever forgive me?" The son looked at his father for a moment and broke into tears. Then his father wept, his mother began crying and the barriers began to fall. It took some seventeen years for the father and son to become acquainted. They have beautifully found one of the greatest gifts in life—one another.

God wants to change some relationships, but only if you are willing to go through a breaking process. Do you know anyone with whom you should have a better relationship? A mother, father, brother, sister...or your spouse?

Now one step from the top—Step 7, you must **give**

God all rights to your life (James 4:13-14). "Go to now, ye that say, Today or tomorrow we will go into such a city and continue there a year, and buy and sell, and get gain: Whereas ye know not what shall be on the morrow. For what is your life? It is even a vapour that appeareth for a little time, and then vanisheth away." Do you realize how much we live life from a future perspective? This is not necessarily bad because we all live some on the "hope" principle. I **hope** things will be better tomorrow. I **hope** tomorrow to have a new house...a new car....I hope...I hope.

But God wants you to give up total rights to any material, psychological or spiritual possessions you have. God wants you to give Him total ownership of everything that is yours. That means you do not own anything, not a suit of clothes, not a car. God owns it all. And this involves an attitude of will.

One evening, our Youth for Christ board chairman came up to me and gave me an envelope. He said, "Duane, my wife and I have prayerfully had you on our minds. We feel God would have us give you this gift. This is not to go back into Youth for Christ. This is not to be part of your salary. It is a gift from my wife and I to you."

During the first year of involvement with Youth for Christ, my total salary was $250. The following year my total salary was $1,000. Just the night before my wife and I had sat down with our bills, right around Christmas time, and our total indebtedness came to $1,000. As a matter of fact, our little boy was two years old and we were convinced that the hospital was going to come get him for back payments. No one knew the amount of our indebtedness except my wife, myself...and the Lord.

We had our board meeting (actually a "bored" meeting!). Then I went home. The board chairman had said that I should open the envelope with my wife. We did precisely that. I opened the envelope thinking optimistically that it might be a check for $50 or perhaps $100.

In that envelope was a check for $1,000. My wife cried.

When I used to hear stories like this I was super skeptical. Yet the Bible says God owns the cattle on a thousand hills and that He will do exceeding abundantly above anything we could ask or think. God has it all. We do not have anything but what He loans to us. It is all His. So many of us grudgingly give back to the Lord, thinking we own something.

God wants your will. God wants that house, that spouse—everything you claim as your own. God wants you to give Him total ownership. When you come to that point, you will have a very different outlook on your home and family.

Our children see these patterns in our lives. Our children can become strong-willed with no concept of what it means to be humble, clean or broken; with no understanding of submission or resistance. Consequently, our homes become the products of all our failures.

We're at the top of the steps. Step 8, **your will must become His will**. Each of us should be challenged to look at our will before the Lord.

"For you ought to say, if the Lord wills, we shall live to do this or that..." (James 4:15).

If the Lord wills. Lord willing. I used to think it was some super-spiritual person who used the term "Lord willing." Well, we should. We are here only by the grace of God.

Many turn this around and say, "If it be the Lord's will I will go to Africa," or, "If it be the Lord's will I will change my life."

What God really wants is for us to say, "Not my will, but thine be done." He wants you to take your hands off your life and let Him run it for you.

That is a prerequisite for anything else as far as family life principles are concerned. God must have your will. Does He?

Lord...let it happen, is my prayer.

Questions - Test Yourself

1. The _____4th_____ chapter of James gives to us a step-by-step breakdown of how God changes the will.

2. The first step in the modification of our will is to recognize its _____inadequacy_____ by itself. *4-1-3*

3. Humility is understanding who we are in relationship to _____God_____ .

4. The human will is defined by analyzing those things to which we _____resist_____ and those things we _____submit_____ (James 4:7).

5. In becoming clean, we must "cleanse our _____hands_____ and purify our _____hearts_____ " (James 4:8).

6. The heartaches, struggles, and weeping that comprise life are God's way of _____breaking us_____ (James 4:9).

7. According to James 4:11, the hardest "member" for God to control is the _____tongue_____ .

8. One of the hardest steps in dissolving the human will is giving God all _____right_____ to your life (James 4:13-14).

9. I know I have experienced real commitment to God and to others when my will becomes _____his will_____ .

10. We should strive to work into our vocabularies

the expression, "See you tomorrow, Lord *willing.*"

Questions for Thought
1. Do you consider yourself a strong-willed or weak-willed person? What factors have established that?
2. Do you agree or disagree with the statement, "Many people do not want to dissolve their differences"?
3. How can proper understanding of the will dimension stymie arguments and confrontations in the family?
4. How do we "submit to God"? How do we "resist the devil"?
5. Can you see experiences in your life that would reflect God's attempt at breaking or refining your will?

7

Watching Those Gauges

Dealing With Pressures

It has been rightly said that we don't trip over mountains. We trip over pebbles. Ever get a stone caught in your shoe? The drip of a leaky faucet can "drive you crazy." These small pressures grow and Grow and GROW!

Dynamite comes in small packages. Consider the atom bomb—it starts with the universe's smallest particles.

In the same way, small troubles at home can sever relationships. "Little foxes spoil the vines" (Song of Solomon 2:15). Sometimes, a particular mannerism of a loved one can become so annoying that after a while it completely controls our thoughts. All we can see are the idiosyncrasies.

In high school I read a story I will never, never forget. It concerned a doctor whose wife was portrayed as bring perfect in every way, beautiful in appearance and charming in personality. She had one small flaw, however, a very small mole on the side of her head. Her husband was a surgeon. Every time he looked at his wife, he didn't see the beauty of her personality or the warmth of her affection. All he saw was the little mole. So he started talking to his wife about the possibility of an operation to remove the mole. Through pages and pages, the author skillfully developed the conflict between the doctor and his wife over this tiny mole. Finally, almost in desperation, the wife said, "Okay, if you feel the mole must be removed, I'll let you do it." Again, page followed page and finally the story concluded...

"...And the doctor operated on his wife, and she died."

Sometimes we can see beauty and good in someone, but the flaws, the little things, become so compulsive and blown out of proportion that after a while, the whole relationship is marred. This is not only true in marriages, but in other areas of life as well. Think of today. Maybe your boss tried to "encourage" you more harshly than you thought necessary. Those children...I wonder if they ever "try your patience?"

Pressures...pressures. They come to all of us.

Irritations and pressures will only be as much of a threat to us as we make them. Sometimes the pressures bear in, and indeed, little foxes spoil the vines. After a while we cannot think straight and our logic becomes short-circuited. Consequently, our effectiveness as people and as Christians is curtailed by these pressures.

Let's consider three types of pressures with which we can all identify: psychological, economic, and spiritual.

Let us delve into the **psychological.** Have you ever felt depressed, lonely or frustrated? Have you ever said to yourself, "Why in the world did God make me this way? Is He merely trying to show me He is boss?" Possible rationale for these feelings is that we need to realize our need for someone bigger than ourselves. We need to see what God is in comparison to what we are.

In college a professor presented the concept of the "bashed image." It has nothing to do with someone punching you in the nose. Rather, it relates to self-image, what you think of yourself. "Bashed" means that to some extent your self-image is incomplete.

"Bashed Image"

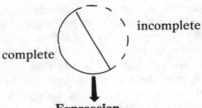

complete / incomplete

Expression
1. loneliness
2. depression
3. anxiety
4. frustration

Action
1. alcoholic
2. suicidal

The broken circle represents "us." It includes our families, our backgrounds, etc. Due to a number of "X" factors, a certain part of us is "complete" (solid line) and a certain part of us is

111

"incomplete" (broken line). Because we all come from difficult backgrounds, each person's circle will be different.

good family,
good education,
good religious background,
etc.

poor family
poor education,
poor religious background,
etc.

In proportion to the incompleteness within us, we will "feel" frustration, depression, anxiety and loneliness. Everyone can relate to these feelings. But the question is, how intensely? The theory of the "bashed image" goes on to say that in accord with the strength of these feelings there will be actions or activities. Therefore, a person with great loneliness might feel pressured to alcoholism, or a person who is extremely depressed might become suicidal.

Thus, the action (suicide) relates to the expression (depression) which relates to the degree of incompleteness (bashed image).

If you want to get an idea of your bashed image, take a long look at your actions. Is your life one of frustration and depression? Do you rely on tranquilizers and drugs? Or, giving yourself to these expressions, do you talk about suicide? Then what you are really doing is reacting to psychological pressures, pressures that are part of life. Now, if all of this interests you from a psychological perspective, what about the impact of Matthew

5:48? Christ said, "Be ye complete as your Father in heaven is complete." Obviously, what God is trying to do is to bring each one of us to a point of completeness, to a point of realizing our full potential as persons, to the place where our circles are complete. He is trying to close them in. Therefore, when we talk about pressures, whatever the problem may be, we should see it as an opportunity. It is something God is allowing in our lives to move us along that **process** of refinement. If only we could have the discernment to observe it as a "process." Being human, we weigh most instances on immediacy—now. But be patient—God is not done with us yet. If we could only believe this and live accordingly.

Another pressure is economic. We seem to live in a world of alternating depression, recession and inflation. It is like the son who went to college and promptly became broke. All he had was enough money to send a telegram home which said, "No mon, no fun, your son." His dad certainly had a sense of humor because he sent back this reply: "Too bad, my lad, your dad."

Economic pressures are real, and again, everyone thinks at times that he might like to have more money. Personally, with one wife, five children, one dog, one cat, two hamsters (the last time I checked), one bird, and one turtle, I stay broke. I have not had a savings account since I was married. It has been estimated that it takes $75 thousand to raise one child. Counting all the animals, I must have at least a $400,000 investment at home. A few of you may have to struggle with what you would like to do with your thousands or millions, but most of us have to deal with mere survival. Most of us are trying to

113

untangle the mortgages and figure out the interest rates. Wouldn't it be nice to have all the money you need just so you wouldn't have to think about it?

Economic pressures are a very real part of life. This problem is not unique to this century. In Proverbs 2:1-5 Solomon speaks to the problem: "My son, **if** thou wilt receive my words, and **if** thou wilt hide my commandments with thee: and **if** thou wilt incline thine ear to wisdom, and **if** thou wilt apply thine heart to understanding, yea, **if** thou criest after knowledge (how many of us cry after knowledge?), **if** thou liftest up thy voice for understanding, and **if** thou seekest her as silver, and **if** thou searchest for her as for hidden treasure, then (conclusion) **Thou shalt understand the fear of the Lord, and find the knowledge of God.**"

How would you like to possess verse five? How would you like to understand the fear of the Lord? How would you like to understand what you are in relationship to what God is? How would you like to find the knowledge of God and be able to identify with the mind of God? That is beyond any comprehension! And notice just before the conclusion: "If thou seekest for her as silver, and searchest for her as for hidden treasure...."

Let's put this in the right perspective. A young minister, wanting to motivate his congregation some Sunday morning, simply states, "Folks, I have hidden five ten dollar bills in the hymn books. The first people to find the money may have it." You can imagine the result.

You begin to see how we have become subconsciously entangled, how we search for silver. "Search for her as for silver, and as for hidden treasure." It's an attitude.

114

I wonder if we try to compete financially? Do you find that the substance of many arguments in your home is financial? God wants us to realize that He will supply all of our needs. "But my God shall supply all your needs according to His riches in glory by Christ Jesus" (Philippians 4:19).

I recall once when the Christian organization that I direct encountered some financial difficulties. One of our Board members said, "Duane, I guess we will just have to ask the Lord to kill another cow."

And I said, "Just what does killing another cow have to do with our financial problems?"

He replied, "Doesn't the Scripture say that God will supply all our needs according to His riches in glory, and doesn't it say that the cattle on a thousand hills are His?"

I had to say yes.

"Well, then," my friend continued, "let's ask the Lord to kill another cow. He knows the needs and that they are legitimate. Therefore, He is going to take care of us."

Whether we die with a dollar or a million, we are still dead. Money is merely a means to an end. If God is real to you, He is going to take care of you, so do not become uptight about economic pressures.

Another pressure is spiritual. Perhaps we feel guilty because we do not have the depth of prayer or devotional life we think we should. The church sometimes creates pressures. Many times, churches try to become the Holy Spirit, rather than letting the Holy Spirit speak to us. We are told exactly how to act, exactly what to say when we pray publicly, and we feel an **obligation** to pick up the Bible and read it before we go to bed.

This is not God's pattern. The Lord wants us to

worship in "spirit and in truth" (John 4:24). Even pastors sometimes create spiritual struggles as they approach the impossible task of trying to reproduce themselves.

Psalm 119:103 states, "How sweet are thy words to my taste, sweeter than honey to my mouth." If we have a choice between being physically and spiritually fed, which do we choose? Many of us look as though we have not pushed away from the table very many times. David is saying in Psalm 119 that his desire for God's Word even surpasses his desire for physical food. The 131st verse of the same Psalm states, "I opened my mouth and panted, for I longed for thy commandments." Can you really say that you have **panted for God's Word?**

The spiritual pressures that are created are the by-products, not of what God meant to happen, but of our inability to really discern institutional Christianity. We have many people who go to church and feel that is religion. I am glad that religion and spiritual pressures can be alleviated if we understand the right type of motivation and meditation concerning God's Word. Psalm 119:97 declares, "Oh how I love thy law. It is my meditation all the day." David's total being was directed toward God. His prayers expressed his desire to approach His Heavenly Father. That should be the way we feel.

Praise the Lord, He gives insight as to **how we should deal with pressures**. Philippians 4:4-7 says: "Rejoice in the Lord alway: and again, I say, Rejoice. Let your forbearance (moderation) be known unto all men. The Lord is at hand. In nothing be anxious; but in everything by prayer and supplication with thanksgiving let your requests be made known unto God. And the peace of God which passeth all understanding shall guard your hearts and thoughts through Christ Jesus."

There are internal, external and eternal facets to these verses. Obviously, if you are going to be able to deal with pressures, you must have the right attitude **internally**. "You've got to have it all together," as the younger generation says. Christ said "...where your treasure is, there will your heart be also" (Matthew 6:21).

Philippians 4:4 states, "Rejoice in the Lord alway: and again, I say, rejoice." How is it possible for someone to always be in a state of joy? Well, it is only possible through the Lord. It is possible if your confidence in God's design and care for you is so emphatic that it overshadows the circumstances. You can rejoice! In Acts 16 Paul was arrested and thrown into prison. His clothes were stripped from him, he was beaten and put into stocks in an inner prison. Imagine the natural reaction: "Lord, why? Why? There must be some mistake."

When I first read this, I thought my first reaction would have been, "Why Lord?" Talk about pressures! Please note Paul's reaction in Acts 16:25: "...Paul and Silas prayed and sang praises unto God: and the prisoners heard them." Thank you, Lord, for the stripes. Thank you for the clothes being taken from my back. Thank you for the oozing blood; thank you for the dingy prison. And he meant it! He really could, in all things, give thanks. Philippians 4:11 says, "...I have learned, in whatsoever state I am, therein to be content." That's the power to grasp.

During seminary, I pastored a small church in Lowell, Massachusetts, and there had the privilege

117

of knowing a Mrs. Alstrom. She was up in years, always smiling, and had arthritis so bad she could hardly walk. Sunday by Sunday she would make her way up to the sanctuary of the church, and step by step as she climbed you could see the reflection of pain on her face. One Sunday in particular I noted the agony as she dragged one foot at a time, step by step, up the stairs. I took her hand.

"That must be awfully painful," I sympathized.

Her response: "Oh, no, oh no. After all, it really isn't my pain; it's God's pain. He's just allowing me to feel it."

That was Mrs. Alstrom; that was the Apostle Paul. In Philippians 4:4 Paul states, "Rejoice in the Lord alway: and again, I say rejoice." Tradition relates that the epistles of I & II Timothy were written by Paul in a foot of water. As much as we strive to understand the truth, one thing is certain—Paul had grasped a power to enable him to meet problems and pressures.

I have jokingly responded, "Never a problem—just an opportunity." But this is seriously a tenet of my personal philosophy. As the external pressures come, they demand some type of internal response.

From the internal, let's view the **external**.

We're going to dissect some Biblical principles as found in Philippians 4:4-7 at this point.

Principle #1—**Develop a predictable personality**. "Let your moderation be known unto all men," says verse five. It concerns how others see us. We can tell much about ourselves and how we react to pressures by stepping back and saying, "What do other people think of me?" When the Lord says, "Let your moderation be known unto all men, the Lord is at hand," He is really saying, "When people look at

118

your life, do they see a person of consistency?"

I know I have gone through some real changes in my life. At one time, when crises or pressures came, I had a tendency to fall apart. I managed to hide it pretty well outwardly. Inside, I was really churning. But the pressures are external. Therefore, the interpretation must begin there. Elsewhere in this book we relate the principle that "no person, situation, problem, or circumstance has to be any more of a threat than we make it." The 51st Psalm says that our inward struggles are manifested externally (Psalm 51:8). The flushed face, the nervous twitch, the coldness in the hands are a few such characteristics.

If we learn how to deal with pressures, people will be drawn to us. "Look at the composure. They seem to have it together so well." How is it possible?

Applying this to a home situation, husbands and wives learn certain patterns about their spouses. Therefore, if you can develop a secure and predictable pattern, it will certainly help to promote a strong relationship.

Tragically, many of us are up and down. We are moody. We say we are not in the mood to do this or that. Is that the way we should be, tossed to and fro? Psychologically, this is referred to as the cycloid personality, up and down, over and about—a roller coaster type of existence. One day this type of person is on a mountaintop, the next in the valley. We really need to come to the point where the valleys are mountaintops, and then the mountains are sheer ecstasy. The only way this can happen is for us to realize that God is in control. That happens to be our next point.

Principle #2—**God is in control**. The Philippians

text gives the reason: "The Lord is at hand. Be careful for nothing" (Philippians 4:4-6). This is King James for, "Don't panic...God is in control." Such faith, yes. But to the rational mind, there is no better objectivity. If God is big enough to create, then He is big enough to give purpose and design to each individual life. The death you did not understand, **He does**. The heartache you did not understand, **He does**. The struggles...your spouse...your children... **He does**.

If the hairs of our heads are numbered, and if we are joint heirs with Christ; if we are saints, set apart; if we have joint citizenship in heaven; if God is concerned and has put His hand on our lives...then we can realize that God is in control, just as the Bible tells us.

I recall a counselling session in which a girl said to me, "How can you tell me God is in control of my life?" She told about a situation with an alcoholic father who came home one Thanksgiving evening after her mother had prepared a lovely meal. The father had been drinking and he proceeded to take the corner of the tablecloth, give it a jerk, and pull the whole meal onto the floor. With tears running down her cheeks, the girl said, "And my father grabbed my mother and forced her to eat off the floor in the presence of all of the children."

We can become the product of adverse situations and turn out the same way as our parents. We can beat our kids because we were beaten. We can become alcoholics because our parents were alcoholics. But through the Lord we have the power to conquer the worst of sins and live above all of these things.

God has established a perfect pattern for each of

us. The excitement is in the **eternal** aspects of Philippians 4:4-9. Notice again God's way to deal with pressures: "In everything by prayer and supplication with thanksgiving let your requests be known unto God" (verse 6). There's a three-p concept in that verse: praise, petition and prayer. The way we deal with pressures is to take our burdens to the Lord and leave them there.

While going to seminary, it was my joy to minister to an elderly lady who had spent no less than twenty-five years of her life in an institution for the elderly. During the last ten years of her life she had been bedridden. One day when she asked me how things were, I started to complain. Please note, I was the pastor; she was in bed. She reached up, took my hand and said, "Pastor, don't you believe you are supposed to take your burdens to the Lord and leave them there?"

I said, "Yes."

"Then why are you taking them back upon yourself?" she asked. I will never forget the thought.

When a problem comes, it is not yours, but God's. Move it up the ladder through prayer. You say, "All right, Lord, here it is." That's really what verse six says. "In everything with prayer and supplication." Supplication is petition.

"Lord, here I am, remember me." But notice, before you present the petition you wave the flag of praise a little bit—with thanksgiving. We should always begin our prayers with an attitude of praise. If you have never tried this, you might try it today. When your head hits the pillow, start reliving the entire day, praising the Lord for everything that went on. Thank Him for all of the good and thank

Him for all of the bad. Thank Him for life and for the privilege of being able to speak.

And after you have gotten into His "good graces," and I say that facetiously, you might say, "Oh, by the way, I do have a couple of things I do not understand. Why is there this sickness? Or why my job, or..." In doing this, you are going through the channels God has prepared to deal with your pressures. If you like alliteration, you have four p's—pressures, praise, prayer and petition. That is the **eternal** quality and that is why God created the relationship between Himself and us.

Still dealing with the p's, notice the conclusion in verse seven: "And the peace of God, which passeth all understanding, shall guard your hearts and thoughts through Christ Jesus." This is the goal: the peace which passes all understanding. What we want psychologically is peace and inner freedom. How much inner peace do we have? The peace of God? You can never find true peace at the bottom of any bottle, or in drugs, or in any other external, physical way. Never, never, never. People do not take flasks of milk to football games. They take flasks of vodka. Why? Because that beverage is more than a beverage to them. But the only way we can really know God's peace is through the pattern established for us in Philippians 4:4-7.

Pressures, then, have an interpretive balance. It is never what happens; it is only how we define what happens.

We all have our own "tolerance ratio" of how much pressure we can absorb. The major purpose of this chapter has been to attempt to bring the pressures to the outside for observation, and then to be willing to change both internally and externally.

Key

"Lord, help me to be able to define my pressures, to be objective in understanding them, and to be willing to change."

Questions - Test Yourself

1. The concept of the bashed image says that all of us, to some extent, are *incomplete*. P-111

2. The four expressions of the bashed image are *Loneliness, Depression, Anxiety* and *Frustration* P-111

3. We know from Matthew 5:48 that God's desire for us is that we might be *Complete* P-113

4. Three different types of pressures mentioned in this chapter are: *psychological*, *economic* -113, and *Spiritual* P-116.

5. According to John 4:24, God wants us to worship in *Spirit* and *Truth* P-116

6. Acts chapter *16* deals with Paul's P-117 imprisonment.

7. In Philippians 4:11, Paul was able to say that in whatever state he found himself, he could be *Content*. P-117

8. We should work hard to have a personality that is *Consistency*. P-119

9. Philippians 4:4-6 makes it clear to us that God is in *Control* P-120

10. Three key concepts set forth in Philippians 4:6 are *praise*, *petition* and *prayer*. P-121

Questions for Thought

1. What is the biggest area of pressure in your life? Discuss.

2. What factors do you feel are keeping you from becoming a "complete person?" Discuss.

3. Discuss the meaning of Proverbs 2:5: "Thou shalt understand the fear of the Lord and find the knowledge of God."

123

4. How do you deal with pressures in your home? Is this easy or hard?
5. In your mind, what is the correlation between prayer and pressure?

8

Keeping the Revs Up

Sex In Marriage

Sex in marriage. I vote a hearty yea! I am for it. Sex was established by God as a relatively natural part of marriage, but many times the bed becomes the battlefield.

A lady called me in tears. "Do I have to have sex with him whenever he wants it? He is so rough; it seems to be only animalistic to him, and frankly, I feel like I am being used. Sex to me is repulsive. It has no meaning."

Hers was certainly a frank, candid and honest outcry. Men can be so subconsciously conditioned by a playboy-hedonistic philsophy that sex becomes "sex for sex's sake." Young ladies indirectly spin off the same struggle. They feel they have to compete with some Hollywood sex symbol, and they can easily move toward the other extreme of repulsiveness.

The whole chemistry of sex is interesting. It will certainly be among the first questions I ask when I get to heaven. We can all look back to our first contacts with the opposite sex. Do so. Think about it. So often, a couple has such an awkward time initiating physical contact. My mother used to say, "Move away from them, not toward them." Now please understand, that was her idea! Most of us have about a six-inch margin around us, and we are very careful about who gets inside. There is a progressive pattern in physical contact. Holding hands will lead to kissing; kissing will lead to necking; necking will lead to petting; and petting will lead to sexual intercourse. This is the normal pattern.

"Daddy, how can I tell if a boy really likes me?" my little girl once asked me. I told her that if a boy really liked her, one of the first things he would do would be to make a move toward her body. She was thirteen years old at the time, and she looked at me as if I had grown an extra head.

"Daddy, what do you mean?" I told her he would start with some nickname and then somehow he would try to get inside that little six-inch margin around her. "He might start poking you or pulling your hair or initiating some type of contact with you."

Her eyes got big as saucers. "Daddy, Daddy, does stomping on the foot count?"

"You bet it does," I responded. "Stomping on the foot is a 'biggie.' "

She related that while sitting around a table at church listening to the youth pastor talk, the boy she liked was sitting next to her. And you guessed it, he was stomping on her foot.

"No question about it, honey," I told my daughter. "What he is trying to do is initiate physical contact. He is subconsciously aware of the differences."

There is always an initial awkwardness in human relationships. To most it is difficult to understand the physical body and how God put us together. No boundaries to the lack of understanding exist. Let me give some examples.

I have counselled with thirteen and fourteen-year-old girls who were becoming mothers. I recall a fourteen-year-old girl who had just given birth to her third child. Incredible, but true. Why? These young people didn't understand the expression of sex—and certainly our society does not help. In most cases this is equally true of the prospective father.

Late one night my doorbell rang. A young couple stepped in. She obviously had been crying. "Something is wrong, let me help," I pleaded.

"I...I just found out I'm pregnant," was her comment. I turned to the boy.

"Oliver, when? How long ago?"

His retort was quick. "How do I know I am the father?"

The girl went into hysterics. "You know blame well you are the father; we have been having sex for two years. You know there have been no others."

They were both fifteen. She had the baby. They were married when they were seventeen.

On the other extreme, I recall a counselling session one evening with a man who was fifty-nine years old. He had a problem of sitting in church and lusting after five old ladies. His thought process would wander from woman to woman. I tried to understand. I am not making light of the struggle. It was real. This man was honestly facing what he knew to be a problem of lust, and it was as real as if he had been thirty-nine, twenty-nine, or nineteen years old.

It is easy to see how we can be affected this way. Our society is "sexually saturated." The newsstand, the movie guide, the conversations of people—it is all around us. It is incredible how our society has built these attitudes into us. "R" and "X"-rated movies and magazines such as **Playboy**—and now **Playgirl**—thrive. I remember seeing a **Playboy** advertisement on the back page of the **Detroit Free Press**. The ad cited the top four monthly subscription magazines and listed their subscription totals. And then it showed **Playboy**, putting out seven or eight million copies monthly. The question raised in the advertisement was: "Where should you put your advertising dollar?"

This doesn't stop in the secular world. I recall being so disturbed with a pastor who left the ministry because he and his wife loved the same woman. The daughter came home from school one day and found her mother in a lesbian relationship with the woman. This is not, of course, true of most pastors and their wives. But here were two people who had committed their lives to each other and to God, but who had driving inner forces that caused them to falter. Before you judge too quickly, think of the words of Christ when he dismantled an entire crowd: "He that is without sin, let him cast the first stone at her" (John 8:7).

How is your sexual life? What fills your mind? What kind of pure or impure thoughts are in your mind on a daily basis? It is sobering to face it as it is—to face what our society has done in shaping our attitudes toward sex. What really is needed is an understanding of God's principles concerning sex. The goal should be to have a mind that is pure, that rises above what this world is subconsciously doing

128

to us. Otherwise, we will become part of the world. We will be a product rather than a catalyst.

Let's examine some Biblical principles concerning sex.

God meant sex to be for the propagation of the human race. I know to many of you that thought is not earthshaking. But it is the first and most obvious principle of sex. Psalm 127:5 talks about God's desire for us to have a quiver that is full. A quiver is the leather sack thrown over the archer's back and used to hold his arrows. A quiver can hold many arrows—we can have many children. My next thought will probably make you "quiver!" According to the **Guiness Book of World Records**, the world's record for births by the same woman is sixty-nine. You ladies might like to challenge that record. Records **are** made to be broken!

Please note that in establishing sex, the continuation of the human existence was God's primary purpose. Somehow we have gotten this out of focus, and our society has twisted these priorities.

A recent newspaper article said that the happiest married people are those who have chosen not to have children. Most parents with large families have thought that way sometimes. When you talk about parents with children, you are talking about added responsibilities, added pressures, and the need for added knowledge. Many parents are just not ready. And there is no question that we reproduce ourselves in our children. We reproduce our idiosyncracies, our struggles, and our needs. Many parents do not realize the problems they create for their children. On top of this, there are many unwanted children who are brought into this world. There are large families with six, seven or eight children. Tragically, as these kids move away from home and church values, the eternal cry is, "Where did I go wrong? Where did I fail?" The mother always hurts a little more. Proverbs 29:15, "The rod and reproof give wisdom; but a child left to himself **bringeth his mother shame**."

A woman was very moved by a sermon and after the service she said to her minister, "Pastor, I feel so stirred by your message. I feel the Lord has called me into full-time Christian work." A very loving pastor looked down and said, "Don't you have a family of eight?" She replied, "Yes, pastor."

And he said, "It's true that the Lord has not only called you into the ministry. He's also given you a congregation." God must give to us wisdom.

If you have children around you, products of the sexual act, there is no question that they are part of God's purpose in giving sexuality to you. We should realize that every child who is born has life-potential. God has a purpose for every life. The role of the parents is to help that child come to the maximum fulfillment of what that sex act represented.

Sex is pleasurable and the Bible says in the book of Hebrews that marriage is honorable. It is important to remember, however, that the overriding reason for our God-given sexuality is to propagate the human race.

A second principle closely aligned with this concept is the realization that **God meant for love to precede sex**. Surveys indicate that ninety percent of married people did not understand love upon being married. When people move toward a relationship without love, they are obviously motivated by either sex or insecurity. "We must be in love, look what we have done," participants in a relationship tell each other.

130

Well, later—in marriage—such couples have to overcome the fornication and sexual involvement that preceded their marriage. They have moved into marriage with suspicion and doubt. That catches up with them psychologically.

In so many marriages, sex precedes love instead of love preceding sex. If two persons love and care for each other, and that relationship moves through the channels God would have it move through, there is no question that sex will in time be the manifestation of that love. Two such people are going to have a desire to give themselves physically to one another. That is the ultimate manifestation of love—or at least, that is the way it should be. Tragically, however, we become caught up in this hedonistic world and somewhere in the relationship, sex is expressed on a pre-marital basis. Then the questions start and the doubts begin. It is important to realize that God not only intended that sex would be for the propagation of the human existence, but also that love would precede sex.

The design of personality is beautiful and complex. We all have consciences. "We shouldn't have done that..." has been expressed by many couples in the back seats of many cars. The comment is interesting as it relates to the awareness of violation of values. I contend that the conscience has two basic by-products: (1.) peace (positive) and (2.) guilt (negative).

Besides the tremor from our consciences, we have drives (sexual), instincts (mating), and senses (touch, etc.). All of this is simply to say that often the hardest dimension to understand in interpersonal relationships is love (emotions). Because of love's importance, a whole chapter has been given in this

131

book to understanding it. The other side is an attempt to lay open the physical dimensions that make this love harder to understand.

When you, Mom and Dad, express yourselves sexually, is it love or sex that motivates you? It is impossible to disengage ourselves from what society has done to us. Maybe we can at least become aware.

Thirdly, **we need to realize that sex can be beautiful**. Even within a Christian framework, we can develop a warped attitude toward sex. I counselled a girl who had been raised by her mother and a spinster aunt. All through her young life she had been told how terrible sex was and how men thought of only one thing—sex. She grew up, felt love toward a particular young man and came to me with a concern. She did not feel she would be able to express herself sexually in marriage. Even though she felt the desire inside to express it, all of her life she had been told that sex was dirty. There is little merit in all the gruesome details, but this girl almost ended up in a mental hospital because of her struggle to realize that sex could be a beautiful experience. God meant it to be beautiful and an expression of love. He meant for sex to take place between two people who really love one another. Proverbs 5:19 speaks about "being ravished always in her love."

A sexual psychosis has developed in the minds of many Christians. They do not believe they can enjoy sex. It is something they have not learned to enjoy and feel they will never learn to enjoy. I am not a doctor or psychiatrist, but as a Christian psychologist, I can say that I think God intended sex to be mutually enjoyable. I counselled a young man who was concerned because he felt his wife had no satisfaction in sex. He would rush toward sexual climax without sufficient foreplay for her to experience climax also. My counsel to him was simply to wait for her. As basic as that was, he called me the next day and said, "Duane, thank you." They had experienced sexual climax together.

And I **must** tell this. There is a "fiftyish" man in Traverse City, Michigan, in "love with me." I have never met him, but I have counselled his wife. His wife was convinced that sex had no meaning. For years there had been no sexual expression. There was no beauty in sex for her. Gradually, her attitude began to change. For the first time, she was seeing in theory that sex could be meaningful for her.

"Why not...go to your husband and express it?" I related.

A week later I got a ten-page letter of thanks **from her husband**. I have never met the man.

"Being ravished always in her love." **Sex is something God meant to be enjoyed.** If you have thought in the past that sex is merely to be tolerated, maybe that is why God has you reading this. If there is not a proper adjustment at this point, it will show up elsewhere in the relationship. If you do not have a happy, secure life as a married couple, then perhaps your communication is poor, too. Perhaps there is real antagonism in each of your roles in the marriage. Frustrations will show up all through the marriage.

Besides realizing that God meant sex to be beautiful, understand that He is the creator of the human body. "And they were both naked, the man and the wife, and they were not ashamed" (Genesis 2:25). God did not mean for us to be ashamed of the

133

human body. At the core of this concept is self-acceptance. Some husbands and wives are "ashamed" of their physical appearance to the point that they do not have freedom of sexual expression. How tragic. We live in a very competitive world. We have let Hollywood establish our mores about beauty. Husbands and wives become subconsciously frustrated because they cannot compete with the Hollywood symbols. A feeling of inadequacy develops. But who in the world gave Hollywood the right to establish a sex symbol? Give me ten billion dollars and five years and I could establish a sex symbol too. I could make fat be beautiful or skinny ravishing. Give me enough money, a large enough base and a generation to pass it onto and I could make anything beautiful. We have really become engulfed by the Hollywood idea that 36-23-36 is beautiful.

God did not make mistakes when he made you. Go home, look in your mirror and say, "There he is," or "There she is...the best looking person in the world!" I mean it! That does not mean we are beautiful by Hollywood's standards, but like all those beautiful and different snowflakes, God meant that nose to be as it is. He meant for those eyes to be as they are. God meant the human body to be something that is accepted.

Sometimes, too much modesty and a lack of self-acceptance lead to real problems in marriage. There's a real difference between being modest and being ridiculous. Some couples feel they have to change clothes in separate rooms. Some husbands and wives are afraid to face each other nude. God meant the human body to be enjoyed. He made sex to be pleasurable. Adam and Eve were not ashamed.

What is your relationship like? How is your marriage in the areas of self-acceptance and sex?

A fifth point to remember is that **God meant for sex to portray oneness**. Look at verses like Genesis 2:24 and Ephesians 5:31. "For this cause shall a man leave father and mother and cleave to his wife and they shall be one flesh." That is what marriage is all about—two people becoming one. The idea of marriage is oneness. One of the greatest compliments that can be given to a couple is, "You know, you almost look alike." They have moved toward oneness to the point that they almost seem to function as one. That is the way God meant marriage to be. Sex is built upon oneness. Two bodies becoming one.

At the risk of being redundant, we need to realize that the woman does not get into the water, swim upstream, lay her eggs and then swim downstream, nor does the male put on his trunks two weeks later, swim upstream and fertilize the eggs. That's what salmon do. Neither do we sit on nests. Please note...it's not done that way. The very act of sexual intercourse indicates what God wanted it to be—oneness. Ephesians 5 compares the union of marriage to that of Christ and the Church. If your sexual life does not manifest oneness—physical, spiritual, and psychological oneness—then real union has not happened.

Satan does have his deceptions. The world really belongs to Satan. The scriptures refer to Satan as the prince of this world's system. There is no area in which Satan can be more victorious than in the area of sex with all of its implications.

Deception is an attempt to fool. Deception connotes trying to make something appear different from

135

what it really is. What a nasty tool! Satan fights dirty. He'll hit below the belt; he'll hit where you are most vulnerable. He'll do anything to win.

Let's analyze the deception of impurity. Galatians 5:22 lists the fruits of the Spirit: "love, joy, peace, patience, kindness, goodness, faithfulness, gentleness and self-control." Please note that the verses preceding this refer to the fruits of the flesh. Flesh is that part of us which is closest to the world. Galatians 5:19 says the fruits of the flesh include adultery, fornication, uncleanness and lasciviousness. Notice that these first four fruits of the flesh concern sex. Satan realized that we are most susceptible to sin in the areas that deal with the sex drive: adultery—taking someone else's wife; fornication—having sexual relations outside of marriage; uncleanness—having an unhealthy attitude toward sex; lasciviousness, or lust—wanting somebody in a purely sexual way. It's ever before us.

It's tragic how the foundations of many of our institutions are wavering. During a family life conference, I had to tell a pastor that two of his deacons were exchanging wives. Even those close to God are vulnerable when it comes to sex. Unless we recognize what is happening, we can easily be destroyed. Even though we live in a society that can put a man on the moon and has the technological know-how to transplant hearts, when it comes to moral fiber we find illegitimate children and venereal disease ever on the rise. Scientists want the absolute in technology. It takes perfect functioning of millions of parts to get that man on the moon. Morality is approached as a relative concept, "Do your own thing...if it feels good do it." I think we've erred.

In many cases, the world has captured us. I John 2:15 says, "...if a man loves the world the love of the Father is not in him." It is interesting to see that God approaches this on an either-or basis. No man can serve two masters. Let's face it—so many fall sexually because our society is permeated with sex. I Corinthians 6:18 admonishes us to flee fornication. I can run toward it or away from it.

I am sure some of you can understand. I do not care how beautiful your secretary is or how handsome that next-door neighbor is. God's exhortation remains, "Flee fornication."

There is more to a relationship than the physical. Some people experience bad marriages because once the honeymoon is over there is nothing else. II Peter 3:3 states, "In the last days there will be many walking after their own lusts."

Why is the sexual part of us so vulnerable? Perhaps it is because we live so close to the world. God has given us spirit, soul and body dimensions. It is the body which is closest to the world. If you want to make a dollar, put a grocery store where none exists. People have to eat. On the other hand, open an adult book store and show dirty movies. Most people are so conditioned sexually that our society pulls the strings and we respond. How tragic.

I remember a course in college called "anatomy and physiology." We saw a film dealing with reproduction. After the class, I was walking across the campus with a girl named Kay. Halfway across the campus she looked up (she was small in stature) and said, "Duane, you know it's interesting that something God meant to be so beautiful can be made so dirty."

Look at your attitudes. Analyze lust, adultery and

uncleanness. Ask yourself how much these things have become a part of your life. God wants you to have a clean mind. Dramatically, Philippians 4:8 states, "Whatsoever things are true, whatsoever things are honest, whatsoever things are just, whatsoever things are pure, whatsoever things are lovely, whatsoever things are of good report; if there be any virtue, and if there be any praise, think on these things." **Think on these things**. We are products of what we think. We are products of our environments. If you give your mind to dirty thoughts, that is what your mind will become.

Another deception that Satan has employed is in the area of **wrong attitudes**. In our society it is easy to develop the attitude of defrauding. The Bible tells us in I Corinthians 7:5 that we are not to defraud one another. Defraud means to use something or someone toward your own end. To me, this means that as a married man with five children, if I use my wife in a sexual manner and look upon her merely as an object to meet my needs, this is defrauding. I am using her for my own gratification. But this works both ways. In situations such as these, the sex act is not an expression of love. Many, many couples crawl into bed and sex becomes a matter of sex for sex's sake, not a matter of sex for love's sake. Sex was meant to be the ultimate expression of love, not an attempt to find it.

If we honestly faced all the times that sex is expressed without love, there would be a minimum amount of sex as the ultimate expression of love. It shows again how the world has influenced us. Is it a matter of using sex to express love or is it a case of defrauding one another?

There is nothing more tragic than for people to toy

with each other's affections. The Purdue Research Poll concluded that the two basic needs we all have are for love and affection, and belonging. We all need affection. God saw that it was not good for man to be alone (Genesis 2:18). I need someone and my wife needs someone, too. Therefore, for any of us to use this area of sex to toy with each other's affections, rather than to express love, can have tragic effects. I Corinthians 7:4 states, "The wife hath not power of her own body, but the husband; and likewise also the husband hath not power of his own body, but the wife." Sometimes the husband will initiate sex—only to hear, "Don't touch me. I don't want anything to do with you." In some marriages, it works just the opposite. The fact that sex is initiated tells us that it is something to be given, something that is needed. We can hope our spouses are sufficiently spiritual not to look elsewhere if we say no, or we can work to make sex mutually enjoyable.

Proverbs 31:11 says, "He hath no need of spoil." The wife has been faithful, she has responded sexually. Toying with affections can have far-reaching consequences. Tearfully a wife related, "Duane, my husband isn't faithful to me. He is involved sexually with someone else." But what about you, wife? Have you put the "sexual cow" out to pasture? If the wife is really able to understand the beautiful chemistry that the Lord has provided her, she can keep her husband coming.

Thus, if there cannot be proper sexual expression in marriage, the problem will manifest itself in other areas. Lack of understanding of love, poor communication, roles of husband and wife, etc. The bed can become the battlefield. Genesis 2:24,

"Therefore shall a man leave his father and his mother, and shall cleave unto his wife, and they shall be one flesh."

Questions - Test Yourself
1. God meant sex for the *propagation* of the human *P.129* race (Psalm 127:5).
2. God meant for *Love* to precede sex. *P.130*
3. The conscience has two by-products, namely *Peace* and *Guilt* . *P.131*
4. A sexual *psychosis* has developed in the minds *p.132* of many Christians.
5. Genesis 2:25, "And they were both naked the man *p.133* and the wife, and they were not *Ashamed* ."
6. According to Genesis 2:24, God meant sex to *p.135* portray *ONeNess* .
7. According to Galatians 5:19, the first five fruits of *p.136* the flesh are sexual sins, namely *Adultery* *Fornication* *Uncleanness* *Lasciviousness (Lust)*
8. We are admonished in I Corinthians 6:18 to flee *p.137* *Fornication* .
P.138 9. To defraud means to *use some one to our own end*
10. Toying with *Affections* can have far-reaching consequences.

Questions for Thought
1. Should sex be expected to be received by husband/wife whenever initiated?
2. "Sex is God's joke upon humanity." React.
3. Love is harder to experience than sex. Agree or disagree.
4. If a couple cannot establish a proper sexual adjustment in marriage, then problems will occur elsewhere in the relationship. Agree or disagree.
5. Was establishing your own sexuality difficult for you? How and why?

9

Those Back Seat Speakers
The Psychology of Raising Children

Nothing is more of a challenge than raising children. It is a full-time commitment from "breath one"—child one. Many of you are saying, "That's for sure!" And every parent, whether or not he realizes it, has a philosophy of child psychology. Each day as you interact in love and in crisis, that philosophy is shaping that child.

Some parents are "**grabbers**"—they grab the child and scream, "I think the devil has hold of you."

And, of course, we all know of the child in this moment of overt aggressiveness who calmly responded, "I do, too. Would you please release me?"

Tragically, many do take out their unresolved conflict and pent-up hostility on their children. Many children become emotional whipping boards and are battered by their parents.

Other parents are **passive.** We live in an era of "progressiveness." Briefly, this philosophy encourages parents to help create an "atmosphere of individuality." Each child's expression and personality can best be developed if he is given the freedom to find it. Therefore, help him to work out his hostilities. Do not stymie feelings. If authority has to be challenged, then so be it.

I had a professor in graduate school, a practicing psychologist, who strongly endorsed this. When hostility came forth between him and his son, he would say, "You hate me, don't you?"

The son replied, "Yes, I hate you."

The father continued, "You want to hurt me?"

"Yes," the son screamed.

"Hit me," said the father.

He did.

I was in class listening to all of this, thinking, the boy is small now but what will he be like when he becomes a young man? "Hit me," says the father, "now help me up and hit me again." This poor, frustrated world desperately reaches for "straws."

Some homes have an **authoritarian** philosophy. One parent makes the decisions. One is dominant. When he or she speaks, the rest listen.

Some of the most "lonely" parents are authoritarian. Deep within they sense that the communication lines are shattered or weak, and in frustration they try to force a relationship. They do not have the perception to realize that they have created the problem because of their dominance. Strong wills breed strong wills.

The best approach is a **democratic** approach. Here the views of all are taken into consideration. This sacrifices neither structure nor "chain of authority."

While in seminary I was on a basketball team that travelled from college to college. We needed the exercise and it was, I hope, good public relations for the school. On one such trip we stayed at the home of one of our team members—way, way back in the hills of Pennsylvania. They had their own sawmill and could hunt elk and wild boar on their property. It was indeed a beautiful location.

Every Saturday morning they had a "family council." All problems or thoughts were placed on an "agenda" on the chalkboard; dad took his place as "moderator." One by one the items were discussed; a vote was taken. Majority ruled. Everyone had an equal vote.

We used to do this at our home on most Thursday nights. We'd go over a passage of Scripture, then consider the items on the agenda. Why not? We do it in our businesses. It sure beats bickering. You have a procedure by which to make decisions. You might try it.

I have been in homes indicative of each of these approaches to child rearing. Sound and clear principles for raising children do exist and I want to attempt to enumerate them. I also want, however, to analyze two areas in which parents fail.

The first and most obvious failure **occurs through ignorance.** Now, this is not malicious. Ignorance means "lack of knowledge." We can only work from what we know and understand. If parents do not **know** the correct principles for raising their children, failure is a strong possibility. Just as I find it difficult to fix my car when it breaks down because I do not **know** mechanical principles, the same is true in many homes as applied to raising children.

Secondly, parents **fail through example.** Many parents expect their children to be something they themselves are not. You can pass along your strengths to your children, but your weaknesses are reproduced as well.

143

What we are psychologically, socially, and spiritually is reproduced in our children. If you have certain habits that you know are wrong, do not be too surprised if these "patterns" crop up in your children. I remember seeing James and Pamela Mason, the English actor and actress, being interviewed on television. They were discussing the smoking problem of their eleven-year-old son. The son had been told by a doctor that if he did not quit smoking, he would be dead within a couple of years.

The interviewer looked at James Mason and said, "Aren't you going to stop him from smoking?"

James Mason looked at the interviewer and said, "No, as a matter of fact, both my wife and I smoke. He heard what the doctor said and how can we expect him not to smoke when we smoke?"

Although I do not condone an eleven-year-old smoking three or four packs of cigarettes each day, at least James and Pamela Mason recognized that it would be hypocritical for them to expect their son to overlook the inconsistency of their comments if they asked him to stop smoking.

It works like this: if you yell and scream around your house, do not be surprised if your children yell and scream. If you upon occasion let loose with some cursing, expect your children to do likewise, especially as they get older. Whatever your pattern of conduct, be assured that in small measure at first, and probably in larger doses later, it will come forth in your children. Psychologists estimate that ninety percent of what a child is comes directly or indirectly from the parents. A child will be involved in church, in a certain social structure, or in peer groups in accordance with the direction in which you lead him. My wife and I concluded that the only cathedral of which we can be sure is the one constructed in our own home. Parents can fail through ignorance and example.

It is an awesome responsibility to raise children by God's Word. These principles are set forth for application. First, **it is the responsibility of the parents to teach the children**.

Deuteronomy 6:7 states, "And thou shalt teach them diligently unto thy children and thou shalt talk with them when thou sittest in thy house and when thou walkest by the way, and when thou liest down and when thou risest up."

As a parent, you must be aware of the **process**, the **product**, and the **person**. In each of these stages, you are a teacher. If you react correctly as your child experiences these stages, later you will most likely be accepted not only as a person, but as a friend.

The above verse presents two principles on how we should teach. We must be **consistent**, and we must **teach with repetition**.

Parents, you must be consistent. The number one reason for children becoming "spoiled" is the lack of consistent discipline.

"They used to think he was spoiled, then they realized that he always smells that way!" This happens when a child subconsciously senses this self-dominant pattern. If, for example, a child is punished for something you have established as being wrong, and the second time the child makes the same miscue the same punishment is not meted out, then an inconsistent pattern has emerged. As a teacher, you must not only define boundaries; within that framework you must also establish an interpretation of ethics. You tell the child what is right and wrong.

145

"When thou walkest in the way, when thou risest up, when thou sittest down." Note the repetition. None of us learned to do an algebraic equation the first time it was presented. No one types effectively the moment he or she sits down at the typewriter. But many parents scream with great passion, "I told you **once**, didn't I?" Children are not responsible and accountable until it is theirs. That means in large measure there must be a slow, deliberate and methodical approach to discipline. It demands perception and discernment on our part.

All the various physical positions are presented in Deuteronomy 6:7 because "it has to be all day long." From the time you get up to the time you go to bed you are a teacher. You are on display.

One of our girls would awaken at 5:30 AM, come into the bedroom and with great conviction bellow, "Time to get up yet?"

As one eye opened, with the other eye still closed, I would "lovingly" and "sweetly" **suggest** that she go back to bed. Yes, my dear friend, it sometimes starts **early** in the morning.

Of course, repetition and consistency are useless if there is nothing to teach. If your children ask concerning your belief in God, or your personal faith in Christ, can you provide an answer? Or instead do you tell the child to go to mother, father, pastor, or priest? We ourselves must know what we believe. The Apostle Paul said in II Timothy 1:12, "For I know whom I have believed, and am persuaded that he is able to keep that which I have committed unto him against that day."

We owe it to our children to have **some** absolute and meaningful conclusions concerning psychological and spiritual values. What parents believe must be lived and should be evident to their children at an early age. Timothy was taught from the time he was a child. "And that from a child thou hast known the holy scriptures which are able to make thee wise unto salvation through faith which is in Christ Jesus" (II Timothy 3:15). Many of us are thankful for wonderful memories of fine Christian parents. Others of us are still striving to overcome childhood traumas and unresolved conflicts.

Do you have a family altar in your home? Dad, are you able to sit down with your family and share the Bible? There is of course the danger of becoming so repetitious that meaning is lost. Remember the maturation of the child. Let me suggest that you take a Bible verse each week and have the whole family learn it. Also that you take a portion of the Bible and have different members of the family respond to each portion as it is presented. I am always amazed at the way my own children reflect, and I am aware that each child must be taught at an early age.

Let us move to our second principle. Besides teaching the child, **the parents also have the responsibility to train the child**.

"Train up a child in the way he should go and when he is old he will not depart from it" (Proverbs 22:6).

Of course, the immediate question is: what is the difference between teaching and training?

Well, it is one thing to have a philosophy of teaching, another to have a method. "Training" in the original Hebrew manuscripts of the Bible conveys the idea of a method. Every football coach has a method of training his players.

As a matter of fact, we have methods of doing most everything. Sometimes we have more pronounced systems of training animals than we do of training

147

children.

After a conference a large, robust, outdoor man came up half smiling, half shaking his head. "Well, you really hit me between the eyes."

"Oh?" With his size, I could not imagine "hitting him between the eyes."

"Yes," he continued. "I remember when I got my first bird dog. I must have read five books on 'How to Train Your Bird Dog.' I have seven children and I have never read any books on raising children."

He was hit between the eyes.

Have you ever sat down with your spouse and talked over methods of child rearing—such as teaching by example? "Train up a child in the way he should go and **when he is old**...." You are not going to see the results of the method as the child is being raised. You are building your children for tomorrow. If you do not see the man as you look at the boy, or the woman as you look at the girl, something is wrong.

I would like to suggest a method. If you do not have a method, try my idea. If you have a better method, let me know so I can tell others about it!

A method connotes purpose and control. Some methods are correct; others are not. They say Vince Lombardi, the former great football coach of the Green Bay Packers, was a hard taskmaster. He was also a winner. He perfected a method and was successful.

Method relates that you sense purpose before actuality. This method is primarily geared for children up to the age of thirteen. It is not for high schoolers.

The first step is **go over the problem and review the consequences**. Whatever the child has done, identify the problem and review the possible consequences. Before anything happens you need to have a response in mind. When the problem does arise, you are not surprised.

Go home, look around your house. Ask, "What would I do if she broke that vase? What would be my response if he came in the back door with muddy shoes?" Remember, every situation is a learning laboratory. Be thankful for the broken vase, thrilled at the muddy shoes. Here's a teaching opportunity.

"Duane, you must be kidding."

No, I have already established that you are the teacher.

Let us use the proverbial cookie jar offense as an example. As a child walks in the door he smells something delicious...chocolate chip cookies. Mom will not be home for a few minutes. The hunger pang says "yes." In Freudian terms, the id says "yes," even though the superego says "no." At any rate, the child walks over to the table, takes two or three cookies, and moves the rest around to make it appear that nothing has been taken (that was my method anyway).

With five children, we have on occasion resorted to the "breath test." Have them all breathe in your face and the chocolate chip cookie villain becomes obvious. Be warned, however, you might have to fight off some bad breath!

When Mother discovers what has occurred, the child is called. Now, assuming that this will be a teaching session, the dialogue might go something like this:

"Did you take the cookies?" asks Mom.

"Yes," replies the child.

"Honey, I do not want you to take the cookies

149

because they are for supper. You will spoil your appetite," states Mom.

Please note the following first step is instructional:

"Since Mom made the cookies you should ask her first, and if you take the cookies again you will get spanked" (note the consequences).

There are many alternatives for consequences. "You will not go out" (denial of privileges). "You will go to your room" (isolation). Weigh the consequences by the **intensity of the offense**, and the **psychological makeup of the individual**.

The second step is called "**feedback number one**." This means that you have the child tell you exactly what you have just said. I think it is a good idea to put the onus on him.

"What did your mother just say?"

"Don't get into the cookies."

"What will happen if you do it again?"

"I will get spanked."

"Why shouldn't you get into the cookies?"

"Because they were made for supper and I will spoil my appetite."

I do not know if your children are anything like mine, but many listen carefully and deliberately. Others have their minds somewhere else during the entire process. You may have to repeat yourself to the child two or three times to make sure the instructional phase is completed.

To **follow through on the consequences** is the third step. If you have said, "If you do that again you will get spanked," be aware that you will have to spank that child. If you have said, "If you do that again you'll have to go to your room for an hour," eventually you will probably have to follow through. So when the child gets into the cookies again, follow through on what you have said.

"What did your mother say would happen if you got into the cookies again?"

"I would get spanked."

We will discuss spanking as a consequence later, but at this point it is imperative to sustain objectivity. What you say in step one you will do in step three.

The fourth step is **"feedback number two" and forgiveness**. After a child has been punished and perhaps some cooling-off time has elapsed, I suggest you go to the child and say, "Do you realize why you were spanked?"

"Yes."

"Why were you spanked?"

"I was spanked because I got into the cookies."

"Why shouldn't you get into the cookies?"

"Because they were made for supper and I will spoil my appetite."

You mean, go through it all again? I sure do. After this you look at the child and say, "Do you have something to tell your mother/father?"

Without fail, my children always have said, "I'm sorry."

You do not say, "Tell me you're sorry." Or, "After all I've done for you..." or "If you really loved your mother...."

Very simply, "Do you have something to tell me?"

Notice that psychologically you are instilling values into your child.

After it is all over I suggest that you take that child in your arms and say, "I love you and I forgive you for what you have done."

That's methodology. Doesn't it beat screaming and yelling and beating? Remember, too, that when they are old they will not depart from it. But parents, it must start with a deliberate method that must be established early, perhaps even before that child is born.

I would encourage you not to be emotionally involved as you discipline your child. The "progressist" states, "The children should know you are angry. We must express, not repress, our feelings." I will attempt to relate another side of that argument. Many times children become an emotional "whipping board" for unresolved problems in parents. Many times over-expression of emotions and too much discipline make strong-willed children.

You might say, "What about Jesus?" There has been much debate about the scene in which Christ threw the merchants out of the temple. He was angry; He was mad. Ever since I ran across the concept called "objective reaction pattern" I decided Jesus was not really angry. Objective reaction pattern states, "Your mind governs your feelings." Thus, you can **raise** your voice, but still be objective and in control. If Christ had said, "Please fellows...I would appreciate it...My father doesn't want His house used to sell merchandise...please" it would not have been nearly so effective.

I could say to my child "Right now I want you to be quiet! Hush!" I could say it strongly, determinedly, deliberately--and if I said it with enough conviction, he would be convinced I was upset. But I might be saying it that way objectively. I could be very much in control.

When a child does something wrong, you can be genuinely upset but absolutely in control of yourself and your actions. It would be great to be in such

152

control of our emotions that in training our children they do not bring out the worst in us.

If you have to raise your voice, fine. Raise it. But be in control. Jesus Christ did not whisper, "Hey, don't use my house as a den of iniquity."

Also, be aware that you should use a **minimum of command**.

"Let your communication be yea, yea and nay, nay" (Matthew 5:37). When you have something to say, say it and shut up.

"When I was your age...." I think there is a tendency for us every time we tell the story to make the distance we walked to school a little longer, and the depth of the snow we walked through a little deeper.

"If I've told you once, I've told you a hundred times...." Most children have a little button behind their right ear that is "turned off" after the word "once."

Remember, we are raising them, not they raising us. Consequently, it is far better for you to say what needs to be said, and then be quiet.

Before we conclude these thoughts on "training," a few words about corporal punishment. Remember, the word is corporal, not capital. I say that tongue-in-cheek, because I have heard many stories of beatings. So many come from a "battered child" background.

I remember a girl who was tackled by her father on the front lawn. The father positioned himself over his daughter to administer a series of blows in succession, right-left-right-left to his daughter's face.

I remember the father who had his teenage daughter strip to her underwear and then administered a series of belt "slashes" across her back. When there was no response, he beat harder, and then his comment to me was, "Why didn't she cry?" He did not understand.

Others were beaten, and then put in closets or put on a leash on the clothesline in the back yard....

A child will identify the pain with the object. If Dad hits the child, it becomes, "Dad hit me." If a paddle hits the child, "I got hit with a paddle." **Be sure that the spanking is firm enough to produce the desired result.**

The book of Proverbs defends corporal punishment. Spanking should be used when there is deliberate disobedience and malicious mischief. A child needs to understand why he or she is being spanked.

If you use the child as a whipping post, do not be surprised if he/she strikes back at you during the teenage years and also becomes very strong-willed. Realize that in the six scriptures in Proverbs in which corporal punishment is mentioned, there is a "rod" used, not a belt. A "rod" was a thin, narrow device used primarily to train and lead animals. Those of you who have had to go out to find a "switch" were probably closest to it. Maybe a fair compromise would be to use a paddle. **Under no circumstances hit a child with your hand, and under no circumstances hit a child in the face.**

My wife is very tender and maternal about it. When she is going to spank one of the children she coils as if she is going to put them in the next country. But somewhere between the coil and the recoil she realizes that this is her child. The maternal instinct begins. By the time contact is made, it is minimal.

Our third general principle is to realize that it is the parents' responsibility to **provide for the children.**

"...for the children ought not to lay up for the parents, but the parents for the children" (II Corinthians 12:14).

I always stand amazed at the way some children have to make it on their own. I feel that if my children want to go to college it is my responsibility to lay away for that day. It is true that throughout high school and college they can pull part of the load themselves. But the major responsibility for the clothes the child wears, the food he eats, the shelter over his head and his education lies with the parents. This is a Biblical principle. So often we rush to make men and women out of boys and girls. At eighteen many are forced out on their own—not only, in many cases, by our society, but by the parents. How many are ready to face life at eighteen?

Finally, our fourth principle is to realize that it is the parents' responsibility to **nurture the child**. "And ye fathers, provoke not your children to wrath: but bring them up in the nurture and admonition of the Lord" (Ephesians 6:4).

How does "nurture" differ from teaching and training? In the original text the connotation is "sensitive to the growth process." However, there must not only be an awareness of the various steps of maturation—namely, impression, expression, and crisis—but nurture connotes also the perception and discernment to deal with that child wherever he is in "growing up." Words like perceive and discern are hard to define. How do you develop an awareness of what the child is **really** trying to communicate? What a responsibility to help him make the **right** decisions. I do believe that development demands awareness. Start, then, by bypassing your immediate reaction to a given discipline situation, and test it a bit before responding. I contend that awareness grows into discernment. Now we are close to "nurturing."

Here are some guidelines to keep in mind related to nurturing:

1. Realize that you must develop in your children what I like to call a **righteous fear**. This is something a little stronger than respect. They must realize that when you firmly say something, you mean it. It is not a matter of instilling fear, but of having a certain strength in what you say. When the children are older and someone asks them what their dad was like, they should say, "When Dad said something he meant it."

2. Realize that **threats are usually worthless**. You must be careful not to develop the impression that you say things you do not mean. "If you do that again, I'm going to give you away." Obviously, that is not so. The child must trust your word.

3. Parents must agree on the **purpose and method of discipline**. Matthew 12:25 gives us the principle that a house divided against itself shall not stand. "Every kingdom divided against itself is brought to desolation; and every city or house divided against itself shall not stand." A child soon realizes how he can pit mother against father. If Mother says "yes" and Dad says "no"—and the child says, "Mom said yes"—an argument between the mother and father usually ensues. Then the child has succeeded. In God's chain of command the wife is over the children. Thus, if my children ask me, let's say, to go somewhere, my immediate response is, "Did you ask your mother?"

"Yes."

"And what did she say?"

"She said no."

"Then why are you asking me?"

If their response is, "She said to ask you," then I understand she wants me to make the decision. I do not cross her decisions when she has made them.

4. **Do not fight or bicker in the presence of the children.** Such an evidence of division can hurt emotionally the child's developmental process.

5. **Realize that your responsibility is to control the children.** I Timothy 3:4 makes it clear that we should rule our own house and that our children should be in subjection to us. "One that ruleth well his own house, having his children in subjection with all gravity." If a teenager is smarter than the parents he will rule the parents and maneuver them to get his own way. If the parents are smarter than the child they will be able to maneuver him. Be tender in the controlling process. "Be ye kind one to another, tender hearted, forgiving one another even as God for Christ's sake has forgiven you" (Ephesians 4:32).

I have had many teenagers come to me and tell me that their mother and father have two different personalities. When they go to church they are such wonderful people and pray so well. But when that parent comes home, he or she is a totally different person, yelling and screaming. Remember, what you are actually like is the way you are at home. You are not fooling anyone if you are the best person in church but go home and use your wife, husband or child as a whipping board.

In the controlling process, if you expect your children to respect your leadership, realize you have to be tender, and show compassion, warmth and love.

You should move slowly in the controlling process.

"We should be slow to speak, swift to hear and slow to wrath" (James 1:19). If a home is confused, it is not unusual to find these words reversed. In many homes the parents are quick to speak, slow to hear and quick to wrath.

I had a young couple come to me after this presentation was given verbally.

"What an awesome responsibility it is to be parents," the wife said.

"Yes, it is," was my response. "We reproduce ourselves."

May God in His tenderness, through his Holy Spirit, make us sensitive to a constant refining process.

Questions - Test Yourself *Passive, authoritarian 142*

1. Three approaches to discipline mentioned in this chapter are: _Teaching_, _Example_, and _Democratic_.

2. Deuteronomy 6:7 presents two principles of *P-145* teaching; we must be _Consistant_, and we must teach with _Repetition_ *Disipline 145*

3. A child is "spoiled" by the lack of _discipline_.

4. To train a child, we must have in our minds a decisive _Method_ _147_ (Proverbs 22:6).

5. Before anything happens in your home, you should have in your mind a definite _Response_ - *149*

6. Many times children become emotional _dumping_ *P-152 bowls* for unresolved problems in the parents.

7. Spanking should be used when there is _Deliberte_ disobedience and _Malicious_ mischief. *154*

8. Overly disciplined children become _self strong willed_. *154*

9. To nurture your child correctly, you must develop in him a _Righteous Fear_. *156*

158

10. It is imperative that parents agree on the *purpose* and *method* of discipline.

Questions for Thought
1. What is the emotional tone of your home? How has it affected your children?
2. Do you have a family altar in your home? If so, is it meaningful? How could it be modified? If not, analyze why not.
3. What is the present method you use for training your children? How is it working?
4. Were you under-disciplined or over-disciplined as a child? Has that pattern continued in your approach to discipline?
5. Why do many parents fail in raising their children correctly?

10

Shifting Gears

Keeping Up With Your Teens

Did you ever begin to dial someone's phone number, only to have that person call you? Sometimes it seems we can anticipate another person's thoughts. Can you imagine anticipating God's thoughts...His design? I would like to suggest that one of the most purposeful pursuits of man is to strive to understand God's thoughts and His principles.

Matthew 7:7-8 states, "Ask and it shall be given you; seek and ye shall find; knock and it shall be opened unto you. For everyone that asketh receiveth, and he that seeketh findeth; and to him that knocketh it shall be opened."

James 1:5 states, "If any of you lack wisdom, let him ask of God who giveth to all men liberally and upbraideth not; and it shall be given him."

My dear friends, if there is an area in which we need wisdom, perception and understanding, it's in being able to give proper direction to our teenagers.

A great heart cry echoes from II Samuel 18:33. After the death of his son Absalom, David laments, "Oh my son Absalom, my son, my son Absalom!"

161

A sense of grief and guilt has gripped many parents. It is a tremendous heartache when a parent finds that his son or daughter is on drugs, is pregnant, or is struggling in some dramatic way.

If your children "go bad," please do not blame the neighbors, the school or the relatives. A large percent of what children are is related to parental training. Let that sit for a moment. It is not my purpose to create guilt feelings, but we must face reality. We **are** responsible for our children. If my teenagers "go bad," I cannot blame anyone but myself. I have been responsible for their instructional pattern. "Train up a child in the way he should go and when he is old, he will not depart from it" (Proverbs 22:6). This establishes two things I must do: (1) break the will but not the spirit ("train"), and (2) be aware of the "bent" of each of my children ("way he should go").

My two oldest girls came home from camp one summer and they were not in the house for twenty minutes when an argument ensued. My wife glanced my way and said, "Duane, does it do any good? We spend money, send them to a Christian camp and as soon as they get home they start arguing."

I responded, "Well, the verse says to train up a child in the way he should go and **when he is OLD** he will not depart from it. Notice, honey, it says when he is old."

Many parents have difficulty seeing the product during the process. We react immediately. One of the overlying themes in this book is "principles, not emotions." When an immediate problem arises, weigh it in terms of the principles, not the chemistry of that moment. What we are actually doing as parents is preparing our children to be independent.

162

What a task! Values, ethics, principles, life-style...
all of this and more to be determined.

**Certainly either the parents are raising the teens or
the teens are raising the parents**. I once observed a
six-year-old raising his parents. This was possible
because the parents did not know how to cope with
the behavioral patterns of their child. It is crucial
that you know how to respond...your thoughts
precede your actions.

One day during my schoolteaching years, a boy
came to me and said, "Mr. Cuthbertson, guess what
happened last night?"

"What happened?"

"I got into a fight with my old man."

"You mean you had an argument with your father,
Dale?"

"No, Mr. Cuthbertson, I had a fight with my old
man."

"You mean a fistfight-type fight?"

"Yeah."

Now if I had ever thought of raising my fist to my
father...I do not even want to think about it.

I said to this boy, "Dale, what was this fight
about?"

"I told my old man he had to sign for a car because
I'm underage. He said he wasn't going to sign and I
said he was. And pretty soon we were toe-to-toe in
the living room."

"What happened?" I asked.

"He beat me up," said Dale. "He's bigger than I
am."

"Then what happened?"

"I went to my room crying. Then after a while there
was a knock at the door."

His father said, "Are you all right?"

Dale didn't answer.

"Will you forgive me?" asked his father.

No answer from Dale.

Finally, his father capitulated. "Dale, if you forgive me, I'll let you have that car."

I looked at Dale and said, "You no-good. You knew you were going to lose that fight before you got into it. You realized there was going to be an argument, that you'd get beat up, go to your room crying and then your dad would come knocking on the door."

Dale said, "Right, Mr. Cuthbertson, but come on out and see my new car."

As I looked out at his bright, shiny new Chevrolet, I realized that Dale was raising his father; his father was not raising him.

Do not go on the premise that your parents did it right. As parents, you bring with you what you are. If you feel that because your dad took his belt, strapped you across the back, and you turned out "all right," then it is "all right" for you to do the same with your children, you are wrong.

I remember counselling a father who in all seriousness told me he had forced his teenage daughter to strip to her underwear, and then had proceeded to use a belt across her back. Without a tinge of understanding, he looked at me and said, "Duane, why didn't she cry?"

I swelled within. How could I explain it? The bitterness, strong will and hostility that was festering within her. But we can only work within what we know and understand. At least he had been willing to ask, "Where did I fail?" And perhaps in some area some of you feel that you've failed, too.

You must be willing to become a student. Let us believe that there is more to learn. If only we could take out of our minds all that we have learned and start anew.

The number one need within your teenager is for a relationship. Your teenager wants a relationship with you.

It's easy to build walls by saying, "I said so, and you're going to do it. I'm your father (or mother). You do what I tell you to do." It's something else to establish a relationship.

The two basic needs of all of us are: [1] love and affection, and [2] a sense of belonging. Look carefully beneath the teen subculture and you will find people who are starved for relationships and affection. This is part of the reason for the parked cars and the backseat love scenes. This is also part of the reason for the drugs and identity symbols. Teens are saying, "Here I am. Look at **me!** Please, can you look beyond the obvious and see **me...me**?"

Psychologically, this is called the **identity crisis**. Teenagers are trying to find themselves. Look at the books that are written for college students. They are constantly asked, "Who am I? Where am I going? What's life all about?" That is why books by Gordon Allport, Paul Tournier and Francis Schaeffer, to mention a few, are so well received.

Mom and Dad, are you going to be there during the struggles? Are your teenagers going to be able to come to you and say, "Mom, Dad, I've got a problem. I don't understand. Help me."

Most teenagers, when they come out of the stage of wanting to become professional baseball players or movie stars, are confronted with some shocking realities. Many teenagers, after faltering on grades, are still searching for identity and want to become rock and roll singers, etc. Government scandals can

165

disillusion to the point that the only hope seems to be fantasy. Boy, do they need the lessons you learned from your struggles! They can only be communicated if the relationship is there.

We need to realize that something happens to most adults on their twenty-fifth birthday. Most of us forget we were ever young when we hit that age. Suddenly it is not "us." It's them.

You were a teenager once. Remember? What were your struggles and what kind of fads were in vogue when you were a teenager? The good old days could not have been all that bad, because they are bringing them back. I remember saying, "I'll never wear a fat tie. I like thin ties." Pretty soon I was wearing a fat tie. "I don't care if everybody grows their hair longer, I like brush haircuts." Then I let my hair grow.

We might as well all face the fact that we live in a youth-oriented culture.

When I was in junior high school all the guys were getting their hair curled. I went home one night and said, "Mother, I'd like to have a home permanent." She looked at me in disbelief and so did my father. He must have thought, "I've really got one! My strong, masculine son with curly hair? Never!"

But one night my mother put the "goop" and curlers in my hair and the next day I walked to school with curly hair just like the rest of the boys. I was not about to be left out of the crowd.

The teenage years are very crucial in terms of identity. If you have an eleven, twelve or thirteen-year-old at home, let me give you a suggestion. Get a tape recorder and have him sit down once a year and make a tape of all the struggles he has faced the previous year. Then file it

166

away. One day he will most likely have an eleven, twelve, or thirteen-year-old blossoming teen of his own. Then, as a point of reference, he can go back occasionally to those tapes. You cannot beat your own voice, your own struggles, for a therapeutic resource. We have a tendency to measure the struggles as adults, not in the light of the years in which they were faced.

Today's youth face pressures we never had. This excludes technological advances.

When I was in high school, drugs were not prevalent. Kids might get stoned on alcohol...but not on drugs.

So-called R and X-rated movies did not exist. If a girl ran around in a film in her underwear, that was racy!

And young women did not face the easy availability of birth control pills.

The situation in which we find ourselves in our society today is a paradox. Scientifically we have gone to the moon and are headed for Mars. Morally, however, we are going down. There is more rape, more venereal disease and more illegitimacy than ever before.

Now, Dad and Mom, transpose yourselves momentarily into that subculture. Before doing so, try to remember your own struggles as a teenager. Recognize that the struggles and pressures on today's youth are more pronounced and intense.

We project our own successes and failures into our children. If you are an athlete (or were) you will probably put into your child's crib a basketball on one side and a football on the other. The child must be an athlete because you were an athlete.

If you were successful academically in college, you

167

will do everything possible to see that your children go to college.

By the same token, your negative patterns of behavior also project into your offspring.

If you cheat on your income tax, expect your children to do the same. If the church is a drag to you, they will probably respond in the same fashion. If you drop them off at Sunday School and then play nine holes of golf, be aware that when your son and daughter hit the teen years they will not be in church.

I once received a phone call from an alarmed bank president. His daughter, who had been one of my students, was in the midst of a pregnancy and was also heavily involved in drugs.

"Mr. Cuthbertson, I am wondering if you would be willing to talk with her," he said. So I made an appointment and talked with his daughter for about two hours. We had a very good conversation in which she said she was rebelling at the structure and values of her home.

I came back to my office and was not there five minutes before the phone rang. It was her father.

"How did it go? Did she say anything? Is there hope?" he wanted to know. Here was a man who lived in the exclusive section of town and wallowed in wealth. He expected me to do in two hours what he had not done in eighteen years. Subconsciously, perhaps, he was acknowledging his own failure.

We are wrong in expecting all of our children to be the same. "I never had that problem with your older brother," we say.

Whether your family is large or small, every child is going to be different. This puts a tremendous responsibility on the parents to raise their children

168

as individuals.

When you say, "I never had that problem with your older brother," or "Your sister was never that way," you are displaying an inability to see your children as individuals.

I would be very weak as an auto mechanic. I know little about cars. I would have to **learn** the science of auto mechanics. Likewise, you cannot understand interpersonal relationships by osmosis; it has to be learned.

We cannot expect our children to be something we are not. By God's grace, sometimes it happens. In most cases, however, the children turn out to be what we as parents are...positive and negative.

Sigmund Freud developed the theory that basically a child goes through three stages. I agree. There are stages of impression, expression and crisis.

The age of **impression** generally takes place in the years from birth through age seven. We are basically "sensual protoplasm." We react, we move. We touch, we taste, we smell, we hear, we see. John Locke drew the analogy of a blank tablet. Each smile, each scream, each joy, each sorrow makes an impression.

I remember talking to a father whose teenage son was an alcoholic. The father told me he used to think it was cute when his son, as a little boy, would take his beer bottle and drink up the final drops. He did not stop to consider that the taste buds are on the tongue, and that taste buds are conditioned. When his son was a toddler the father was making him an alcoholic.

Every parent reading now should ask, "What does my son or daughter see? Taste?" All those little "doors" go into the mind for future interpretation.

When I was young, I thought it was "cute" to walk with one foot slanted to the right. My foot grew that way. Those little habits grow, and we as parents weep.

During those early years, the memory bank is operating and deposits are being made. And we remember. Almost as passive conversation, all of us relate, "Why, I remember going...coming..." "When I was your age...." Those impressions are indelible. Do your children a favor. Give good memories to them. Times with you along...your trip to the ball game, etc. Give to them good memories from your home and vacations.

And what a challenge is the stage of **expression**, ages eight through thirteen. "Why? Why? I know, Mom, but why? Why, Daddy? How come?" After a while you get the feeling that it is really not all that important. It is just a matter of "why?" During the age of expression your child will test and challenge you as much as you will allow. A social consciousness and awareness is developing. It is tragic to say to your child, "Well, you're just dumb. You're stupid. Shame on you." A parent tries to shame the child by calling him or her names. So the child begins believing that he is "clumsy" or "dumb" or whatever. The child becomes caught in these guilt patterns. At this age he is very much affected by the consciousness development.

Social patterns are also important during this stage. This includes the acceptance by one's peer group. (Peer group is **not** those with whom you swim.) We just cannot minimize the trauma of acceptance. It takes much to be different, and many adults fight patterns of change.

During this stage our emotional development

170

becomes more pronounced. We feel love, joy, hate, anger, sorrow, jealousy, anxiety, and fear. How these feelings are developed is extremely crucial. If children are exposed to hate and anger they will more readily express hate and anger. What a challenge to give them an atmosphere of love and joy!

I have always felt that the youth of America should sue the individual who coined the word "puberty." The word almost sounds dirty. Of course, the word reflects that youth is a time of change. Young people become confronted with sex. It is imperative that they are given proper sexual education. I first heard about sex on the streets, and I remember speaking up loudly to the older boys, "No, my father wouldn't do that." Well, he did, and here I am. With the sexual permeation of our society, we had better have both a line of attack to education and a readiness to anticipate questions.

A parent said to me, "My boy was fine until he went into the Army. The Army wrecked him." Nonsense. The Army brought out what he really was. You can put a balloon under pressure and it breaks at the spot of the most obvious flaw. This is true of your life. We bend where we are the weakest.

During the age of **crisis**, teenagers will be asking questions. Parents need to be there. The mother-daughter and father-son relationships are extremely important at this time. It will be a time when woman-to-woman and man-to-man talks are necessary. It is a time for the mother and daughter to go shopping or the father and son to go to the baseball games together.

Let's consider the philosophical struggles of the "age of crisis."

171

Freedom versus structure.

"You have to be home at 10:00 PM." "Tell the lady you are sorry." You have to conform to the structure that has been established by your mother and father, the teen is told.

Obviously, a certain framework of instruction and teaching is necessary. On the other hand, teenagers long for freedom. They have a school situation in which they are supposed to move from class to class. Some students skip a class and then they are obviously caught in the freedom versus structure squeeze. As a parent, you must be aware of this. If you are wise, you will try to help your son or daughter see that there is a purpose to all of the rules and the structure you have built into your home. Otherwise, there will be confrontation.

A friend of mine who was a dean of students at a seminary said, "Freedom is very risky, but it sure produces better products." I have never forgotten his statement. If a teenager cannot come to the point of sensing individuality and freedom in his psychological environment or religious training, then that teenager will consciously or subconsciously rebel. Either is tragic.

A girl I counselled was forced by her parents to go to church twice on Sundays, and also on Wednesday evenings. Obviously, her parents were strict. She had had one date in her entire life and he had to fill out forms in triplicate to get in the door! Her parents were scared that the boy might not measure up to their standards or be of the right spiritual stature.

This girl told me that she would sit through a Sunday evening service so tight, all the while thinking, "If he preaches one minute past the time when I can get home and watch **Bonanza** at 9:00, it's all over for him." So through the entire sermon she was thinking about the time.

Her parents finally said to her, "If you want to go to college, go to a Christian college." She did. In three months she was expelled.

I was involved throughout this whole process and I asked her what happened during those three months. She said that in three months she felt she had to make up for all the time she had been forced into a rigid structure. If she stepped out of line at home, a Bible verse was quoted to her.

So at college, she was "liberated." She related, among other things, that one night she got so drunk that she fell down a flight of stairs and ended up in the hospital. She had her first sexual experience. It was not something she wanted. But she felt it was one of the many experiences she had been robbed of having. "I've got to make up for lost time." Getting away from home was national liberation day for her.

Another girl said to me once, "Duane, I don't want to be too religious because I'm afraid I might miss something."

If there is no balance between freedom and structure, that is exactly the way your teenagers will feel. They will feel that they are somehow being cheated out of life. The religious experience in your house must be something that is lived and practiced. It must be vital and alive, not just a Sunday thing. It must pulsate through your total being and life. "You shall know the truth and the truth shall make you free" (John 8:32). Has your religion bound you, or does it release you? In order for your teenager to see it, it must be a releasing process.

Conformity versus individualism.

We live in a world of mass conformity. As adults,

173

we have made it this way. If you are a teacher, engineer, or factory worker, you have established a frame of reference for yourself. But a teenager is still trying to find himself. There is no way to measure the conforming pressure of a peer group, a school system, or a society. The world's hedonistic philosophy does not help. If a teenager is not involved with a member of the opposite sex or has not taken drugs, he or she is not "with it" (supposedly). The teenager has to see purpose in being an individual and in standing up as an individual.

I remember a boy whose father was a university professor coming to me for counselling. Throughout his house the boy was always exposed to pornography and girly magazines. The father was constantly pushing these on the boy. In the boy's mind it was totally obnoxious.

"Am I really different?" the boy asked me. "I don't have any desire to shack up with every girl I see. My father thinks I'm weird." This was confronted by the concept of what his father thought a sharp, educated, enlightened individual should be. He was trying to get his son to conform to this mold.

The atmosphere of your home should enable your teenager to find himself as an individual. I repeat: the atmosphere of your home should enable your teenager to find himself as an individual. God did not mean for the home to be a "filling station." Come in...fill up...go out. The home is that unique laboratory that God meant for development and growth.

Home values versus social values.

Parents can become "uptight" when social values, school, or peer values conflict with home values.

A young man wanted to lead a rock and roll group and stay out half of the night practicing. The parents said, "No, you must be home, go to church, and help out with the chores." Finally after embittered confrontation, society won and he ended up leading a rock and roll band. The parents sensed failure.

You have to realize that the home values you have established are going to be tested during the age of crisis. They are going to be. So prepare yourself. Don't be too alarmed. Do not become too uptight if your son grows long hair and your daughter wants to conform to certain social trends. If you do, you are going to lose. Even if you win, you lose. You may be able to forcefully mold them, but as you do, they will turn against you.

One father used to be very concerned about his son's long hair. He would come to the dinner table and make cracks about the "girl" sitting across from him. The boy would sit in silence.

"Be careful you don't get your hair in your food. Who's the young lady at our table tonight?" the father would say.

The son came to the point where he detested his father. I talked to both of them and told the father that he must see his son as an individual.

"You must see him in terms of the crisis he is going through," I told the father.

The father was a good student and one night he made this little speech to his son.

"Son, I want you to know that even if you grow your hair down to your feet, I still love you. I apologize for making such an issue of your hair."

It was well received. Two days later the son had his hair cut. What the boy had been saying was, "That's what I wanted to hear, Dad. See me as a person and

175

then I will conform to the values you have set for me."

As humans our rituals for freedom differ from other animals. No mother chases her son up a tree and abandons him. Neither do we have girls literally kicked out of the nest. No...in case you did not know.

However, around the age of eighteen, most young people are thrust into society. Some go into military service, some go to college, but our society in large measure assumes...**assumes** they are ready. It might be well to stimulate some reader's imagination to propose for our society a measurement of maturity and independence quite distinct from physical age maturation.

Teenagers want to be independent, to make decisions, and to really feel that their judgment is heard and followed.

If you are a wise parent you will be aware of these struggles. I know of no teens who at the age of thirteen or fifteen want to be totally independent. They are glad their parents assume responsibility for food and housing. They do want to be independent, however, in terms of such things as driving the car and curfew time at night.

I remember when I was fifteen I told my father one afternoon, "Dad, I think I can drive the car."

My father looked at me and said, "You think you can drive the car?"

"Yes, I've watched you drive and I think I can do it."

So he pulled the car over and put me behind the wheel.

I thought, "If that's the way he is going to be, I'll show him."

I turned the engine on, put it into first...and

realized something for the very first time. I discovered there was a very delicate balance between the clutch and the accelerator.

I put the accelerator down and let the clutch up. The car stalled. A little more nervous, I tried again, and killed the motor a second time...a third, a fourth, a fifth time. My dad sat there nonchalantly watching me kill the motor time after time.

When I finally got the car moving, I was so nervous I reached for the door handle and screamed, "I'm getting out!"

But my father reached over, grabbed my arm and said, "No, son, you're staying right here."

My father eventually helped me learn to drive. Please note...he was smart enough to let me try. People just do not become independent; they have to be directed. Then you, parent, have to recognize what those struggles represent.

You see, the issue was not really driving the car. As a young man I was testing my wings, expressing that I wanted to be recognized as a man. As a parent you must be sensitive to these struggles. You went through them, too.

If you want to determine whether you are successfully making it with your teenager, go through this check list:

First, **how does your teenager respond to your discipline?** "Correction is grievous to him that forsaketh the way; he that hateth reproof shall die" (Proverbs 15:10).

I always insist on eye-to-eye contact with my children so I can see how they are responding as I am admonishing.

Second, **note how they talk back, or perish the thought, curse you**. "Whoso curseth his father or

177

mother, his lamp shall be put out in obscure darkness" (Proverbs 20:20). If your children are talking back excessively, cursing you or saying things behind your back, realize the warning signal.

Third, **analyze the situation carefully when they decide to set their wills against your will**. "He that being often reproved hardeneth his neck, shall suddenly be destroyed, and that without remedy" (Proverbs 29:1). When we get our blood pressures up, generally our faces become flushed and our necks become rigid. Does that occur at your house?

Fourth, **be sensitive to whether they feel you owe them something**. If they take from you, and they can steal from others and feel justified in so doing, a major problem is before you. This is obviously a critical sign. "Whoso robbeth his father or his mother, and saith, it is no transgression, the same is the companion of a destroyer" (Proverbs 28:24).

If you happen to be religious and your teenager wants to hurt you, he knows the greatest pain comes when he says, "I don't want to go to Sunday School. It's boring. I'm not getting up. It's a drag." That hurts! If it comes to that point, it means they want to see the pain and to see you getting hurt.

Fifth, **if the home is insecure, they will have a desire to stay away from you**. In stable and secure homes, there is enjoyment in being together. I do not believe in the generation gap. In secure relationships, the children will be there to get their questions answered. Some teens, of course, have an excessive desire to be away from home; they are "ashamed of" and want to "chase away" their parents.

"He that wasteth his father and chaseth away his mother is a son that causes shame" (Proverbs

19:26). Certain children continuously want to be away from their parents.

Sixth, **the heartache comes when the children are older and still delight in seeing their parents hurt**. "Despise not thy mother when she is old" (Proverbs 23:22).

I hope all of this helps you to recognize the struggles that your teenage sons and daughters are having. God wants us to be reconciled to one another. He has given us the ministry of reconciliation (II Corinthians 5:18). Reconciliation means "closing the gap." Maybe you, Mom and Dad, need to have a closer relationship. Go now and start the process. God wants there to be a relationship, whether it is among your brothers and sisters in the church or among the members of your family. If there is animosity, bitterness or resentment, God wants a reconciling experience to take place.

Questions—Test Yourself

1. If our teenagers go bad, we must recognize the major responsibility is _____ .
2. The two basic needs we all have are the needs for _____ and _____ .
3. Something happens to most adults around the ____ birthday.
4. We project our _____ and our _____ onto our children.
5. Three pressures today's young people face that most adults did not have to face are _____ , _____ and _____ .
6. Three stages of a child's maturation are:
    a) the age of _____
    b) the age of _____

c) the age of_____
7. Four philosophical struggles of the teen years are:
    a)_____
    b)_____
    c)_____
    d)_____
8. The first danger signal that you are failing as a parent is that your teenager is not responding well to your _____ (Proverbs 15:10).
9. If a teenager wants to hurt a Christian parent, he knows one of the easiest ways to do so is to have no desire to attend _____ .
10. The ultimate heartache comes when the children are older and still _____ (Proverbs 23:22).

Questions for Thought
1. How is it possible for children to raise parents? If this happens, how have the parents failed?
2. What are some of the end results when teenagers are not given love and affection and a sense of belonging?
3. Can you relate some of your own identity struggles during your teen years? Why do we forget so easily?
4. Of the four philosophical struggles mentioned in this chapter, which one do you personally relate to the most? Why?
5. Why is it so difficult for parents and teens to reconcile (close the gap) after barriers have been established?

Other HORIZON HOUSE books you will enjoy

TO YOUR KITCHEN...WITH LOVE by Barbara Schaefer. This beautiful, spiral-bound cookbook is a delightful collection of tasty recipes compiled by a missionary mother for her bride-to-be daughter. Timely devotional thoughts sprinkled throughout. Diet section included. 117 pages, paper, $3.95.

THE TAMING OF MOLLY by Molly Clark is the author's own account of how God came into her life and changed her. A story of spiritual and physical healing, "backsliding," and progress. Humorous, warm, and helpful. 96 pages, paper, $1.50.

CRISIS AT 9:25 by Barry Moore is a collection of hard-hitting messages by an international evangelist from London, Canada. Pointed and provocative. 95 pages, paper, $1.75.

HELP FOR HUSBANDS (AND WIVES!) edited by Eric Mills comes with a definite masculine appeal, but has loads of help for ladies too. A series of nine unusual accounts that includes contributions from authors Pete Gillquist, Richard H. Harvey and R. Stanley Tam. 92 pages, paper, $1.75.

70 YEARS OF MIRACLES by Richard H. Harvey is the amazing account of the miraculous in the author's own life. Dr. Harvey's impeccable credentials and lifetime of integrity qualify him to write some unusual things. One you won't want to miss! 192 pages, paper, $2.50.

WHAT WILL YOU HAVE TO DRINK? by Jerry G. Dunn with Bernard Palmer. Observing the growing acceptance of alcohol by many of today's evangelicals, the authors search the scriptures and examine the issues involved. 110 pages, paper, $2.50.

EVOLUTION: ITS COLLAPSE IN VIEW? by Henry Hiebert examines the teaching of evolution and finds several crucial areas in which the famous theory simply cannot face the facts of modern science. 171 pages, paper, $2.50.

THE BUSHMAN AND THE SPIRITS by Barney Lacendre as told to Owen Salway is the fascinating life story of a former Indian witch doctor, his conversion to Christ, his experiences with witchcraft, and his ministry for the Lord. 185 pages, paper, $2.95.

FIBBER'S FABLES by Richard H. Boytim. The time-honored fables of Aesop retold in a bright, new format. Complete with biblical applications. Great for kids! 96 pages, $1.75.

ALIVE AND FREE by Marney Patterson. This Anglican evangelist has come up with another Horizon title which reveals the heart of his international message and ministry. Pictures throughout. 160 pages, paper, $2.50.

MY GOD CAN DO ANYTHING! by Clarence Shrier is an amazing account of God's healing intervention in one man's life. Some stories are just incredible—this one is true. 96 pages, paper, $1.50.

TALL TALES THAT ARE TRUE by British Columbia Storyteller Arthur H. Townsend. A fascinating collection of crisply written short stories with spiritual applications. "A Million Dollar Bonfire," "The Pig Was Insured" and many others. An excellent gift. 96 pages, paper, $1.95.

VALLEY OF SHADOWS by Jake Plett. When his wife MaryAnn was abducted and murdered near Edmonton, Alberta, Jake and his two small sons went through seven months of agony and distress. It became an odyssey of faith. Very inspiring. 170 pages, paper, $1.95.

CRIMINAL FOREVER, by Gary Ziehl as told to Merribeth E. Olson. Gary Ziehl was an habitual criminal for whom no hope was held. But for fear of the hangman's noose he might have killed. But since his dramatic conversion, the law's somber prophecy that he would be a criminal forever has been proven wholly untrue. 96 pages, paper, $1.95.

HOW TO SET GOALS AND REALLY REACH THEM by Mark Lee. Dr. Lee, dynamic president of San Francisco's Simpson College, makes an enthusiastic case for goal-setting, then goes one step further and shows how to really reach those objectives. 95 pages, trade size, cloth ($5.95) or paper ($2.95).

CHOCOLATE CAKE AND ONIONS....WITH LOVE by Marilynne E. Foster is a collection of recipes that she has discovered in her own use to be tasty and easy to prepare. The love comes in selected excerpts from various writings on the theme of love. 96 pages, paper, spiral spine, $1.95.

THE SHEPHERD'S PSALM and other true accounts edited by Eric Mills. Exciting insights into one of the world's favorite pieces of literature (Psalm 23) plus "The Flask that Wouldn't Break," "A Broken Home and a Broken Heart" and more. (Formerly entitled **Preachers, Priests, and Critters**.) 93 pages, paper, $1.95.

TREASURES IN HEAVEN by Beatrice Sundbo is a warm, human look at how the author faced the deaths of four of her family, then her own death. Inspiring and triumphant. 96 pages, paper, $1.75.

DARE TO SHARE by Marney Patterson. Sub-titled "Communicating the Good News" this is an encouraging handbook on relating the Christian faith to others. Affirms that God's Word does not return void and those sharing it (whether from person to person or from the pulpit) should expect results. 122 pages, paper, $1.95

I ESCAPED THE HOLOCAUST by A.M. Weinberger as told to Muriel Leeson. The incredible story of the author's abduction by the Nazis during W.W. II as a young rabbi, his torture in Nazi labor camps and his dramatic escape from extermination. The story of his pilgrimage from Judaism to atheism to Christianity. 96 pages, paper, $1.95.

A LARGER CHRISTIAN LIFE by A.B. Simpson is much more than devotional material from another generation. It is an eloquent philosophical statement from one of the most influential men ever to serve Christ. 160 pages, paper, $2.95.

I WISH YOU COULD MEET MY MOM AND DAD by Tom Allen. What makes a 23-year-old son brag on his mom and dad? And why do his nine brothers and sisters feel the very same way? Humorous, helpful and inspiring. 121 pages, trade size, paper, $2.95.

UFOs: SATANIC TERROR by Basil Tyson. Around the world an estimated six UFOs are sighted every hour. Tyson's explanation is both startling and impressive. 116 pages, paper, $1.95.

DAM BREAK IN GEORGIA by K. Neill Foster with Eric Mills. At 1:30 a.m., Nov. 6, 1977, the dam above Toccoa Falls College burst, sending 176 million gallons of water raging through the sleeping campus and taking 39 lives. The story behind the headlines. A dramatic account of Christian victory in the face of tragedy. Introduction by Rosalynn Carter. 160 pages, trade paper, $2.95.

BEYOND THE TANGLED MOUNTAIN by Douglas C. Percy is an authentic African novel by an award-winning Canadian author. From his pen spins a fascinating web of missionary heroism, romance, tension, and tragedy. Douglas Percy is one of the "best" on Africa. First time in paperback. 158 pages, paper, $1.95.

BORN AGAIN: WHAT IT REALLY MEANS by Alain Choiquier. This old term, once muttered in embarrassment, has now invaded Madison Avenue. Its true meaning is admirably explained by French preacher Choiquier. 400,000 in print in French, now for the first time in English. 51 pages, paper, shrinkwrap pack of six for $4.75, the price of five. Not sold separately by the publisher.